PRAISE FOR *NO LOOSE SCREWS*

"Compelling, hilarious, moving, honest—I found this memoir hard to put down."

—**Katherine Catmull,** author of *Summer and Bird*

"Byers speaks with an effervescent voice in her strikingly real memoir…Don't pass this book up."

—**Martha Louise Hunter,** author *Painting Juliana*

"We need those surviving souls who have walked through the fire before us. Deena Byers has not only done so, but can articulate what it was like with rare wit and grace. In "No Loose Screws," she remembers not only the difficult and trying, the frightening and dehumanizing parts, but the parts shot through with comedy, beauty and wonder. Her memoir deserves a place on your shelf—better yet, in your hands."

—**Jesse Sublett,** author of *Never the Same Again*

"Byers connects with her readers. Challenges, successes, joys and sorrows—we all share her journey. Her humor, pathos, and wit appeal to audiences of all ages. Enjoy these timeless and universal truths."

—**Rose Potter,** Faculty, UTeach-Liberal Arts,
The University of Texas at Austin

a memoir

NO LOOSE SCREWS

and other true stories

Deena Byers

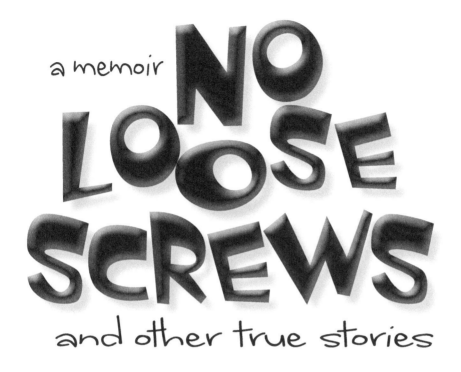

No Loose Screws and Other True Stores
A Memoir
© 2015 by Deena Byers

ISBN: 978-0-692-51473-3
Library of Congress Control Number: 2015954296

Profits from this book's sales will be donated to Women for Women
International, a non-profit organization that helps women survivors
of war rebuild their lives.

The events described within this memoir are the author's personal
thoughts and recollections. The dialogue is written to the best of the
author's recount of the events that took place.

Book Cover and Text Design by Rebecca Byrd Arthur.

DaVinci & Co. Press
Printed in the United States of America

I want to thank everyone who has touched my life,
except for Mother Superior, who punished me
for eating two helpings of mashed potatoes.

Table of Contents

a memoir

NO LOOSE SCREWS

and other true stories

Prologue

*M*y writing coach, Annie, said emphatically, "I don't ever want to read another frickin' bulleted list again! These are stories about your life, not a bunch of business memos. Show me what happened; don't tell me. Dig deep into your thoughts, your feelings, and take me there. Be vulnerable. You got it?"

I didn't welcome these talking-tos from Annie, but heeded her straight-forward advice. I had no choice but to obey. Annie did not mince words. An author and storyteller, she dubbed herself, "The Evil Memoir Coach," which I thought true after one of these tough sessions.

Switching from years of communicating in corporate lingo to writing in story form took a lot of practice. I'd start a story only to fall back into writing an objective business memo. Sometimes I'd just write over and over again, "I want to write this memoir and I can do it. I will let my readers know my deep emotions during the ups and downs of my life."

I did a lot of research to verify my memories. I talked to my family, friends, and relatives about events in the past. I poured through court records and newspaper articles. I searched through piles of diaries and photos. I'd revise my first draft time and time again until each story brought my experiences to life. If I was successful, Annie would say, "You did it. I'm so proud of you. I felt like I was right there in the moment with you."

Her sparsely doled out compliments didn't totally relieve my angst or those days that my brain just couldn't access words, no matter how hard I'd try. Still I kept writing—some days only a few pages, other days a completely new draft that didn't pass Annie's keen scrutiny. "Rewrite this. I want more detail. Expand on this comment. Make this story come alive more. What made you feel the way you felt?"

I experienced a huge range of emotions while writing my stories. I was incredibly sad while working on "Our Father," a story about the saddest and scariest times in my childhood and "The IV League," a support group in which we expose our fears and vulnerabilities. However, I laughed out loud writing "Crime Scene in The Kitchen" and "My Drug Dictionary." When I wrote "The Judge's Verdict," I felt proud that I took a firm stand on an issue that ended up benefiting an entire community.

My love of words and writing kept me going. I gained a greater perspective on my life through this process, a benefit I hadn't expected. I learned that each part made me who I am today: a grateful, resilient, happy person. ❁

The Cazenovia Carousel

*T*hey seemed to fly ever so lightly. One by one, I watched the carousel horses twirling round and round, like huge fireflies illuminating the evening sky. The bright lights on the canopy flashed in rhythm with the calliope music, the cadence pounding in my bones. The memory of riding the painted horses is still alive.

The colors and lights were so lively and bright.

Growing up in Cazenovia—a tiny rural town nestled in the rolling hills of Wisconsin, with a population of 325, four bars, two grocery stores, a gas station, a post office, a bank, and a funeral home—my twin brother and I spent months every year waiting for the traveling fair to come to town in August. Each year, we treasured the one quarter a piece Dad handed us to spend at the carnival. Though Dad made good money as a skilled electrician, he seldom gave us any unless we worked for it. Days in advance, Gerry and I talked about everything we would see and do at the carnival with our quarters, enough for each of us to have our own seat on three rides. Every year, we'd select our same favorite rides: the carousel, Ferris wheel, and flying swings.

The year we turned nine, quarters in hand, we took off for the carnival. As I swung my arms back and forth on the way to the park, the quarter suddenly flew out of my hand and landed somewhere near a deep ditch in tall thick grass. I couldn't believe it! We searched and searched until late in the day. Devastated, we gave up hunting after an hour or so and decided to find Dad and ask for another.

We headed straight to the bars in town, where we knew he spent his time on weekend evenings. Sure enough, we found him in Manville's Tavern, sitting on a swivel barstool, smoking Camels in his light gray work shirt and dark gray work pants. We figured Dad would give me another quarter, if for no other reason than to look good in front of his bar buddies, who were laughing at his jokes and drinking a free round on him. Instead, Dad shot me the meanest look, his eyes fiery, and said in a low, gruff voice,

"Get the hell out of here! I already gave you a quarter!"

We bolted out of the bar. We sat on the grass near the carousel watching it circle in front of us time and time again. With only a quarter between us, we no longer could have our own seat on three rides. We decided to pick our own carousel horses and hoped we could share a seat on another ride. We checked out every horse, their colors, sizes, and stances. I wanted a horse with a big bushy tail. One horse, painted red, yellow, and green, had a warm smile, friendly brown eyes and front legs stretched out high in the air, head tilted toward me. "That's the one I'm riding," I said.

My horse galloped up and down on the carousel as my ponytail flew back and forth in the wind. I held my arms high in the air, balancing myself on the stirrups, shouting to Gerry, "I'm flying! I'm flying!" Gerry smiled from the horse next to me, but didn't say anything because he knew if he opened his mouth, he might swallow bugs when the wind blew.

I imagined my horse flying me to faraway places with skyscrapers, museums, and fancy restaurants. I imagined flying to the countries Sister Kathleen taught us about in our geography class, places like France, Italy, Greece, and Africa. I imagined riding on carousels in big cities and traveling all over the world, meeting people from other places, and seeing wild animals roam in their own habitat. I wanted to swim in an ocean with sky-blue water, not dark brown mucky water like in our town lake.

The ride ended much too soon. With only one ride left between us, I started to cry. Gerry said, "You can take the ride. I'll watch you." No way would I leave him behind. I told the carnival guy operating the flying swings that we were twins and I had lost my quarter. We had only one ticket left and no money. I'll always remember his chiseled, worn face with the chipped decaying teeth, looking at us sadly and then saying, "There are empty swings right now. I'll let you both have your own swing." We gave him our ticket. On cloud nine, we soared high out and up over the people on the ground on our swings, saying, "I'm flying, I'm flying."

Not wanting the magic to end, we wandered through the carnival with night approaching fast. We smelled the pink sugary cotton candy, the sizzling hot dogs, and the funnel cakes topped with powdered sugar. We listened to the fast-talking carnival barkers enticing people to their game booths to win one of the huge stuffed teddy bears hanging from the white sidewalls. Gerry saw me gazing at a big black one, with white feet and a red ribbon and said, "I wish we had more money and could play the darts and could win a big stuffed animal to share."

Once dark fell, we lay down on a grassy area, holding hands and looked up at the millions of bright stars that peppered the sky and together said,

A view of Cazenovia, Wisconsin

"Star light, star bright, first star I see tonight. I wish I may I wish I might, have the wish I wish tonight."

We walked home hand-in-hand, wanting another wish to come true. We hoped Dad wouldn't be home yet because after a night of drinking, his meanness came out. We wanted to avoid him. If we were lucky, we might be able to sneak in the kitchen door and quietly go upstairs to our bedrooms.

When Dad was drunk, he couldn't climb the steep stairs. If we heard him coming up the steps, we hid in the attic holding our breath, quiet as church mice, until he stumbled back down. We heard him snoring and rushed upstairs to our beds. I curled up in a safe cocoon and pulled the covers over my head. I wished I could fly away. ❀

Gerald and Geraldine

Two peas in a pod

$f$rantically waking my twin brother in the middle of the night, I whispered, "Gerry, please go with me now." Without hesitation, we put on winter coats over our flannel pajamas and slipped into rubber-soled bunny carpet slippers to venture outside in the dark.

The biting January cold in rural Wisconsin smacked us in the face. We'd walked the sloping path so many times, knowing the exact number of steps to get from our house to the wooden, shingled-roof outhouse–forty-three steps–all the while holding hands to keep from falling on the icy dirt-worn path. Afraid of the dark and the boogeyman, I felt safe with Gerry.

Slipping down the path to the two-holer, I flipped the light switch on. "Deena," Gerry whispered, "Don't you wish Dad was a plumber instead of an electrician? When we have our own houses, let's have indoor bathrooms with real toilet paper, not catalog pages." Shutting the thatched wooden door, which never closed all the way, he patiently waited outside, freezing.

We were born four days after Christmas, and Ma didn't expect twins until Dr. Rouse proclaimed, "I see another baby." There I came fifteen minutes later. Being two months premature, together we weighed about nine pounds. When we finally arrived home from the hospital, Ma couldn't bathe us in water because our skin was so thin it would crack. Instead, she used baby oil.

Since we were sixth and seventh in our family of eight children, my ten-year-old sister, Louise, took charge of looking after me. Anita, eight years old, took care of Gerry. Ma, always at home, instructed my sisters how to care for us. An easygoing baby, Gerry seldom cried. As for me, I usually screamed when I wanted something.

Though fraternal, we had a strong twin connection from birth. Gerry and I had an unspoken communication between us. Without saying, we didn't tattle on each other—maybe at times on our brothers and sisters, but never on each other. We would often be introduced to strangers as "the twins." So when asked our names, we would say together, "the twins" and giggle.

As first-graders in Catholic school, we went by our nicknames, Gerry and Gerrydina, not our birth names, Gerald and Geraldine. Usually I was the last one in the class to finish printing my full name on the blue-dotted-line paper, prompting Sister Kathleen to say, "Aren't you finished yet?" I hated being the last one.

One day, on our mile walk home from school, we came up with a plan to split Gerrydina in half. Gerry would still be G-E-R-R-Y. I would be Dina, but change the spelling to D-E-E-N-A. That way, I could shorten Geraldine to only five letters and we could print our names in the same amount of time. Today, Deena is on important documents, including my passport and driver's license, though my mother called me Geraldine until the day she died.

Gerry and I loved putting on make-believe weddings with my brothers and sisters playing a part. Usually, I'd be the bride and Gerry the groom, with my little brother, Bobby, the best man and sister, Janie, the maid of honor. My older siblings, Louise, Anita, Junior, and Anna, would be the priest, bridesmaids and groomsmen.

Staging the weddings on our large front lawn, I'd wrap a big white sheet around me for my wedding dress, pin a lightweight cheesecloth in my hair for my veil, and carry a bouquet of the white lilies-of-the-valley that grew in droves all around the outside of our house and had the sweetest fragrance. Neighbor kids joined us, and everyone would sing, "Here Comes the Bride" as I walked down an imaginary aisle. Ma would watch us from the kitchen window, smiling while she was baking pies.

As kids, Gerry and I were inseparable. We had our own twin language. We lived in our world and did everything together. "Deena, we're two peas in a pod, just like the two peas in this pod I'm shelling. Isn't it nice having a built-in friend like we do?" I'd nod in agreement and we'd both laugh. We would play games we made up, pick apples from our orchard, gather our homegrown vegetables and fruit to sell door-to-door. We were attached at the hip, seldom without the other. Over the years, as we grew up, we often discussed how lucky we were to have each other to lean on during a difficult home life with no luxuries.

Gerry and me holding our older sister's twins

We were the only two in our family to get college degrees, coincidentally both in Journalism. I attended the University of Wisconsin-Madison in the late 60s, while Gerry was in the Navy, and he attended the University of Wisconsin-Whitewater in early the 70s. Financial aid made it possible for us to accomplish this; Gerry received a subsidy from the GI Bill for his Vietnam service, and I

Gerry home on leave
from the Navy

earned a four-year academic scholarship. In addition, we took out government loans and worked several jobs through college. I cleaned houses, waitressed, and go-go danced at a college bar. Gerry bagged groceries and worked at a 7UP factory. I remember being exhausted and stressed, ending up in the hospital a couple of times for ulcerative colitis. I was determined to do whatever it took to get a degree to eventually become an executive in business. I still have a recurring dream that I missed my finals and didn't graduate. To comfort myself, I framed my diploma and hung it on a wall in my home office.

We each had our own idiosyncrasies. Mine had to do with toilet paper. I did not like using slippery pages from Sears, Spiegel, and Montgomery Ward catalogs. Today, I keep an extra stash of thirty-six mega-rolls of the softest, most absorbent toilet paper in my bathrooms.

Gerry was fascinated with Christmas lights. One year, at age eleven, we had no gifts under the tree because they hadn't arrived in the mail on time from Spiegel Catalog. Making the day worse, Dad blamed Ma and they got in a huge fight. Topping that, to our dismay, the only three strands of lights on our little tabletop Christmas tree all burnt out. Gerry, who seldom got upset, cried and said, "When I grow up I want to have a lot of lights, so if some burn out, I can still have a bright Christmas."

Gerry now puts up forty to fifty thousand lights almost every year. He says, "I'm so excited with all my lights. I have happy Christmases, unlike the sad ones I remember we had as kids." The local Tulsa stations feature his sparkling animated outdoor Griswold-style electric splendor displays. One time, he had red, white, and blue lights blinking to patriotic music honoring Americans who served in war, while a lively spectacle of Santa's reindeer pranced on the rooftop. Tongue in cheek, he says, "Deena, my hand gets really tired from signing autographs for all the people who line up to see my lights."

Just a few of the 40,000 Christmas lights on Gerry's house

Every year on our birthday, Gerry calls me and starts the conversation with a corny joke.

"Deena, a guy in choir asked me today, 'Gerry, is something wrong?'" I said, 'I'm sad because my twin sister will forget my birthday.'" We laugh knowing that is impossible.

"Gerry, when people ask me my age, I just say, 'Today my twin brother is fifty or whatever.'"

He asks, "Does the person get it?"

I reply, "No. Most just say, 'Wish him a happy birthday.'"

Still laughing, he adds, "Remember Ma telling us 'no one ever promised us a rose garden?' Well, that's why I grew a big one of my own with red, white and yellow roses." We laugh some more. He ends the conversation, "Deena, don't ever forget that when we were born, I held on to you so you would come out with me, but I lost my grip. I'm glad Dr. Rouse found you inside Ma."

Several times, Gerry and I both sent our mother the identical birthday card, without talking to each other in advance. We attribute it to twin sense. During the Vietnam War, Gerry, on weekend furlough from his duties on the USS Forrestal, bought and sent the same card to Ma as the one I bought in Wisconsin. Uncanny!

Another incident still gives me the chills. I was driving Ma to Minneapolis from Cazenovia, when I suddenly blurted out, "Something's happened to Gerry! I can feel he's sad." The minute we walked in the house, the phone rang, and Gerry said crying, "Tracy is gone. She died in the night." At only three months old, his daughter had died of sudden infant death syndrome (SIDS). I felt devastated for him.

I still vividly recall the night I woke up from a horrid nightmare shouting in my college dorm room, "He's on fire! He's on fire!" My roommates told me the next morning they heard on the news that men on his Navy ship had died when a fighter plane landed on the deck and caught fire. Gerry, a quartermaster on the upper deck, saw it all happen, one hundred thirty-four men lost. Though not physically hurt, Gerry had that horrible event etched indelibly in his mind.

For me, our intense twin sense is like a double-edged sword. I like feeling when Gerry is happy, but feeling his pain really hurts. When I have these strong feelings, I know that something is happening to him, and it isn't just in my mind.

Our personalities haven't changed much over the years. I'm as determined and outgoing as ever. Gerry is still easygoing and laissez-faire. He doesn't worry like I do. We call each other often and visit each other when we can. We continue to enjoy making each other laugh. We both know that we would never say nor think anything unkind about the other. Just as I can't imagine growing up without Gerry, I can't imagine a world without him in it. As we often joke, "We knew each other long before we were born." 🌼

Our Father

"You, you, you, and you; number 3, 5, 7, 8. Get outside now!" Dad would proclaim to us Compton kids, "We're moving the outhouse today." Early each fall, our toilet had to be pushed from its current position to a new position over a freshly dug hole, a necessary annual ritual. I detested this task, and reminded myself, *Hold your nose, so you don't have to breathe in the pungent stench. It will be over soon.* Trying not to look directly at the muck, I squinted my eyes and held my breath. I wished we had an indoor bathroom like most of the people had in town.

The Compton family
Back row, left to right: Louise, Anita, Junior, Anna
Front row, left to right: Janie, Gerry, Deena, Bobby

To Dad our names and genders didn't matter, and he often called us by numbers denoting our birth order. Pointing at me, he'd say, "Number 7, after the boys and I get the biffy moved to the new spot, you take that heavy metal rake with the red handle in the shed and help level out the shit. Spread it out evenly and it will make good fertilizer for your Ma's roses." He'd always remind number 5, Janie, to do the worst job—knocking down the piles of frozen poop in the winter.

We jumped when Dad barked any order at us. "Dig ditches, rake leaves, mow the lawn, hoe the garden, pull weeds, plant trees," you name it. If we even looked like we weren't marching to his commands, he'd express his disgust: "You are worthless and won't amount to a hill of beans." To please him, we worked as hard and fast as we could. One after the other, we got our orders to do another chore to avoid a beating right there on the front lawn. Neither our neighbors nor Ma interfered and stopped Dad. They were afraid of him, too.

A skilled electrician, Dad worked out of town during the week in Madison, sixty-seven miles away, and came home Friday night. His hands were strong with thick fingers, callused and rough from years of wiring buildings out in the cold.

On the weekends, Dad would take one of us kids to help him on an electrical job for someone in town. Working with Dad wasn't easy. Since we were all thin and agile we had to crawl into tight spaces. I remember the time Janie said, "I saw a bunch of black and yellow spiders in a cellar today and they were yucky-looking." My brother, Bobby, number 8, said, "I was face to face with big rats in an attic and got the hell out of there, fast." I recall seeing brownish black snakes with a yellow collar slithering along in a dirt cellar. No wonder none of us kids became an electrician.

An earthy sense of humor, Dad could be the funniest, nicest person in the world. He had a good memory for jokes, and would tell us one after another, making us laugh, although sometimes they were crude and not suited for kids. More often than not, he'd be drunk by dinner time and turned into a scary person, clenching his jaws, tightening his eyebrows, and slurring his words as he drank beer after beer.

We knew to stay out of Dad's way, especially when he drank. His behavior became erratic.

Though Dad took out his anger on all eight of us kids, for some reason, my sister Janie, three years older than Gerry and me, received the worst abuse. At twelve, Janie found a stray mama cat, which she cuddled, loved, and nurtured. She contracted ringworm from handling the cat. Because the nuns at school notified my mother, Dad drove Ma and Janie to the doctor in Reedsburg, fifteen miles away. The doctor looked at the back of Janie's head with an ultraviolet light and became visibly upset when he saw a big bald area where hair had been pulled out by the roots. He asked Ma what had happened. I can't imagine what Ma said to the doctor, but I'm sure she couched the truth. Janie went home with medicine cream for her ringworm.

Once Dad beat Janie so hard, she crawled with blood streaming down her legs to the neighbor's house across the street. Someone called the sheriff that time, but seldom did a neighbor get involved. I remember hearing the sheriff shout, "Art, stop hurting that child right now."

Dad said, "You can't tell me what to do. You work for Richland County. You should know after all these years our house is in Sauk County." We lived just across the street from the Richland County line. Even the local sheriff seemed afraid of Dad and didn't want to come near him.

In the late fifties, Janie, at age fourteen, hitchhiked to Milwaukee to be with our older sister, Anita. Rather than have Janie be labeled a juvenile delinquent for running away, Anita took her to the County Courthouse in Milwaukee to be emancipated. With about a hundred signatures obtained from people in Cazenovia, who said they had seen Dad mistreat Janie or one of us kids in one way or another, the judge declared Janie a ward of the State of Wisconsin. She was happy to be free and never came back home to live.

I am haunted by images of Dad stomping on the stomach of my older brother, Junior, hitting my older sister, Anna, so hard in the face that she went to school with black and blue eyes, and rubbing the nose of my four-year-old brother, Bobby, in his own poop for making a mess in his pants. Ma usually stood nearby helpless, pursing her lips and wringing her hands like she couldn't do a thing to make Dad stop. I hated these times, but after Dad went back to work on Monday mornings, she'd say, "The Mister is a mean son-of-a-bitch," one of the few swear words I ever heard her use.

Gerry used to say to me, "You won't get slapped and hit as much if you just quit talking. Keep quiet when Dad yells at you." Gerry kept his mouth shut and didn't sass back. Only when Dad asked him a question did he talk. He didn't get hit as often as the rest of us because of his adroit ability to predict the weather accurately, a talent on which Dad relied because the weather determined when we worked outside.

For hours at a time, Gerry would sit under the wide maple tree next to our garden and look up at the sky. He would keep Dad abreast of the weather, "See that dark cloud coming in from the north and the sky changing to a dark greyish blue? That means it's going to rain here late this afternoon, at the latest by eight o'clock tonight." His predictions were spot on. He still calls me to let me know when a really bad storm is coming my way as he tunes in to several channels simultaneously getting weather updates.

Gerry and me with Ma and Dad

Dad would sit on the front porch of our white two-story frame house with blue shutters, smoking his unfiltered Camel cigarettes, one after another, and gaze over our land, which he referred to as "his plantation" and make sure every area met his specs. The acre or so included a manicured lawn with lush green rolling hills in the background, an apple orchard, and a well-hoed garden full of corn, strawberries, cucumbers, potatoes, and other fruits and veggies. We grew the biggest, most succulent strawberries

I've ever seen in my life and sold them door-to-door for twenty-five cents per quart. At the time, I never realized that growing up on fresh fruits and veggies was so good for my health. I always wanted a candy bar from the store, but Ma couldn't afford it on her meager grocery budget.

Not even once can I remember Dad or Ma saying to any of us "I love you" or tucking us into bed with a goodnight story. In her own German way, I did feel Ma cared about us a lot. Now my brothers, sisters and I give our own kids a lot of attention and tell them that we love them.

Once, at fourteen, before I realized he'd been drinking, I asked Dad to take me to Reedsburg and buy me a pair of school shoes. He screamed, "You can buy your own goddamn pair of shoes. Who do you think you are that I should buy you shoes? Use the money you make taking care of your grandpa after school." His face got red and angry. He looked like the cruel boogey-man I often saw in my dreams. I was scared to death and before I knew what hit me, Dad twisted my arm and broke it. Then he stormed out of the room. I screamed really loud and Ma came and asked me what happened. I cried, "I never want to see Dad again. He hurt my arm." I ran downtown holding my arm and told the Richland County Sheriff what had happened. He called the Sauk County sheriff. Someone from that office came to Cazenovia and drove me to the nearest doctor in Reedsburg.

It had been years since I thought about the extent of Dad's abuse. In 2011, rummaging through an old tin box of things I had kept from my past, I found a letter from my mother. When I read it, I cried. The letter brought back a flood of memories, talking to the social worker, going to court, and telling the judge my dad had broken my arm. The judge asked Ma if my dad beat me and my brothers and sisters. She replied, "Geraldine has a huge imagination." I figured she was afraid to say anything else, fearing the wrath of Dad.

Just like another Wisconsin judge had ruled several years earlier that Janie didn't have to return home, this judge also directed that I would be removed from my parents' custody. Vaguely, I can recall walking out of the courtroom with my social worker and looking at Ma and Dad, who never looked back at me. I felt guilty, scared, and alone.

Reading Ma's letter again, I was struck by her sadness and her lack of an explanation about why she didn't stand up for me in court. Instead, in her beautiful cursive, she wrote,

"Never worry about any wrong you feel has been done to you. That is for the other fellow to worry about. Your only worry is what you may have done others. May your life be strewn with roses, although in this old vale of tears, life just isn't that way. Bye for now, The Poor Excuse of a Mother."

The letter from Ma

Fifty years later, I wanted to know more about how I got to the courthouse in Baraboo, forty-five miles from home. I decided to search for any official records that hopefully still existed. I made many phone calls and wrote letters to various departments of the Sauk County Court. Then one day, I received a call. My file, number 6-51, was still in the archives and it included three years of testimony, evaluations, reports, and judge's orders.

The clerk at the court called me and told me what had happened as I listened intently. The little kid was me that we were discussing, and I felt sad for her. It seems after I went to the doctor in Reedsburg, a lady took me to her house to stay for a few nights. The next day, a social worker came and talked to me. A week later, I went to a court hearing and afterward a social worker

16

took me to stay with a foster family in Plain, Wisconsin, until, a short time later when I went into the convent.

Recently, I asked Gerry to tell me one of his happy childhood memories. He replied, "Gee, I just can't think of one. Do you think there's something wrong with me?"

I said, "Remember when we rode the carousel at the carnival? Were you happy then?"

"I suppose I was happy at the moment, but we always had to go home afterward," he said. "My happiest times were Monday mornings when Dad left town to go back to work. I don't spend time thinking about our childhood. I guess it made me who I am. I feel lucky I have a happy life today."

When I was in my twenties, unexpectedly at the age of sixty, Dad died having a beer at the bar in Alt's Tavern, chain-smoking his Camels, and telling jokes to his buddies. Dad fell off his barstool and a couple guys, sitting at the bar near him, got up and rushed over to him, picked him up from the floor, and lifted him onto the pool table. Dad was unresponsive. One of the men ran to get my mother. He told Ma that Art didn't mention anything hurting him before he fell. When she got to the bar, he was lying on his back on the pool table. Ma said that she had never seen him look so blue in his face. The coroner stated, "Art had a massive heart attack," and concluded Dad had most likely died suddenly when he fell off the barstool.

Since the Catholic Church would not have a ceremony for Dad because he wasn't Catholic, the Methodist Church agreed to conduct one. Dad would have said, "I don't want to be caught dead in a church." We buried Dad in the public cemetery, which sits on the tallest hill overlooking Cazenovia.

Afterward, my brothers, sisters, and cousins went to Ma's house and gathered around the old upright piano that stood kitty-corner from the couch in the south living room. Ma played and we sang happy songs and shared funny jokes that Dad had told us. I felt guilty that I didn't feel sad he had died. 🏶

Fruit of Thy Womb

All of us kids came home for Ma's 70th birthday.

$\mathcal{W}$ith her wide, warm smile, my mother welcomed guests into our house all the time. When someone dropped by on a weekday morning or afternoon, no matter the milkman, the egg man, the ice cube man, the Jewel Tea man, or the Fuller Brush man, my mother would swing open the screen door and say, "Come on in. Have a chair."

She'd motion the guest to sit on one of the red, vinyl-covered, chrome kitchen chairs and ask, "How's your day going?" Her warmth and hospitality wrapped visitors with love. Giving her full attention, she offered them delicious treats like her freshly baked cinnamon rolls, oatmeal cookies, or a piece of pie with perfect flaky crust she'd made from scratch.

We loved people coming over. It meant we kids could eat the treats too. Ma would say, "If you want to go to a party, start one yourself." To her, most everything called for a party: a birth, a First Communion, a gradu-ation, an achievement, or a soldier's return. She loved having parties and invited everyone: friends, relatives, acquaintances, pen pals, and strang-ers. People referred to her as "Kind Hilda."

Wearing one of her signature floral bib aprons, Ma would give each person a warm hug and make everyone feel comfortable and important.

Her parties started with white paper tablecloths spread out on the picnic tables in the front yard, ready for her home-made food: ham, casseroles, breads, a variety of relishes, and round angel food cakes with swirly meringue frosting colored bright pink, blue, yellow, or green. The parties went late into the night and ended with Ma pounding on the piano, crooning with her exuber-ant alto voice along with the crowd to oldies like "Jealous Heart," "Ain't She Sweet," and "A Little Street Where Old Friends Meet."

The memories are sweet, but every day was not a party at our house. There were days when Ma sat peeling potatoes in the kitchen while Dad beat one of us kids right outside the kitchen on the *Ma always wore a bib apron, except to church.*

lawn. We screamed for help, but she'd peel the potatoes faster and faster, as if she couldn't hear us. I remember the sound of the potato skins slapping against the enamel pan in her lap while my dad hit, slapped, and kicked us. I cried and cried, wondering why she didn't stop him.

A gregarious person, Ma made a wonderful fuss over everyone, but she became painfully silent when Dad went on a rampage. I wondered what attracted her to Dad. She said, "We loved to dance and used to tear up the floor, especially when we did the Charleston and the polka. The Mister was such a good dancer back in the day."

Ma and Dad in the 30s

People often told Ma that she could have been a perfect stand-in for Edith Bunker, a housewife in the seventies TV sitcom *All in the Family*. Like Edith, Ma permed her light brown hair and proudly wore a bib apron over her dress, as if modeling a fashion trend. She made her aprons on our manual treadle Singer sewing machine out of cotton flour sacks with colored flowers. Her favorite one had red daisies and green leaves on a light purple background with white piping borders and two deep wide pockets on each side, also with white piping. Ma wore an apron most of the time, even to the bank, post office and grocery store, but never to church.

Ma also resembled Edith in her mannerisms: she pounded the piano loudly, singing in a cheerful pitchy voice, and scurried obediently to serve Dad when he barked, "Hilda, bring me a beer." Not a drinker or smoker herself, Ma would shoo anyone out of "The Mister's" tattered worn brown easy chair, covered with burnt cigarette holes, so Dad could sit in his chair. Handing him his Schlitz, she'd say in a cheerful voice, "Here you go." Dad would mutter a short grunt, showing his satisfaction. I thought, *Why does Ma act subservient to Dad? And she is so smart. She graduated valedictorian of her high school class.*

Years later, after my first marriage ended, I went into counseling. Laura, my therapist, helped me understand how my relationship with my dad had shaped me and created my beliefs. I had to visualize myself as a child again, with all the intensity and pain. The memories of Dad saying mean things were devastating:

"For every leaf that I find in the lawn, I will pull another hair out of your head."

"The door slams both ways so don't let it hit you in the ass on your way out."

For two years, I met with Laura and struggled to learn how to forgive Dad for abusing and belittling me. Reflecting on my childhood, I hurt all over again. I knew my dad's youth had been horrible, and he had grown up under dreadful circumstances. His dad had died in a ditch from alcoholism and his mother, a mean and angry woman, spent little time with Dad. His mother used to come and visit us when I was little and said awful things to Dad, "Art, you're no good, just like your dad, a mean drunk." I was young when Grandma Harris died and Dad shed no tears. With pitiful role models, I realized Dad did the best he could raising a huge family he never wanted in the first place.

Ma came with me to at least three of my therapy sessions, and I asked her why she didn't protect us when Dad started hitting us. I remember her sitting on the couch with her head hanging down, crying, and saying, "I wanted to keep our family together. If I called the sheriff, you could have all been taken away. Your dad hit me late at night when you kids were sleeping."

Divorce was not an option for Ma, a devout Catholic. My heart hurt for her as I realized that she had also lived in fear of Dad. Still I had a hard time understanding why she didn't tell Dad to hit her instead of us. I think she felt trapped and had nowhere to go, no way to make a living, and no other resources to support eight kids. I remembered how Ma used to throw holy water against the front door on Friday night each week before Dad came home from work, praying on her rosary beads he would be sober.

Dad made the money and he let everyone know that. On Saturday mornings, he'd throw a portion of the cash he'd made that week on the kitchen table and say, "This is yours, Hilda. Pay the bills. And don't spend it all in one place." The money was never enough and Ma had to pinch pennies. He spent the rest of the cash on booze and entertaining his bar buddies.

Though Ma did her imperfect best to hold our family together at any cost, we either ran away, or Dad told us to leave the day we graduated from high school. Dad said, "You know where the roads are and walking ain't crowded."

My therapist asked, "Hilda, is there anything you'd like to say directly to Deena?" Ma apologized and said at the time she didn't know what to do. She said, "I was taught that as a Catholic, a person stays married through thick and thin." I felt her remorse and regret. She felt helpless at the time. She said, "The years after your dad died have been among my happiest years."

Every winter for nine years, Ma lived with me in Minneapolis to help care for my daughter, Jessica. She lavished Jessica with love and attention. Often, when I came home from work, they were singing together at the piano. Ma taught Jessica the lyrics and melodies to her favorite songs as she played them. She spent hours teaching her new words and how to spell them. She encouraged her to read books and write letters, and taught her how to conserve and reuse everything from cards to tinfoil to jars, because this habit saved money. I loved seeing Ma be the mother that I had wanted her to be when I was a child.

Ma at her piano with photos of all us kids displayed on top of it.

Ma's family lived during the Depression, and she had learned to live without luxuries. While raising us eight kids, she recycled everything in her own inventive ways. She cut the margins off magazine pages and the empty space off bills to use for lists and notes. She packed empty cereal boxes with her cinnamon rolls and goodies for people to carry home. She cleaned and reused tinfoil until it cracked and crumbled. We watched her wash out plastic bags and darn holes in worn-out socks. Rags survived passing through the Maytag wringer washing machine until they were practically threadbare. The same Kerr jars were saved and reused for decades. Ma canned anything and everything—rhubarb, peaches, pumpkin, green beans, beets, jam—and stored them in our cold Wisconsin cellar. After her hysterectomy, she even preserved her uterus in a quart jar, which she kept in the cellar, and showed it to anyone who was willing to look. She was so proud of the womb that bore all her children.

Though Ma has been gone for twenty years, I will never forget her parties. My memory of them lives on through her piles of sheet music, the one thing I inherited from her. All the pieces are original, some dating as far back as the early 1900s. Some are in pristine shape, others torn and tattered, with her flowing cursive writing on each stating the date, where she bought them, or the name of the person who gave it to her and their address.

I miss seeing Ma in her gingham bib aprons, sitting at the kitchen table cutting out coupons, reading her daily thoughts, writing pages of single-spaced letters on her old Smith Corona typewriter. I miss her big toothy smile. I miss her loud laughter. I miss hearing her playing the piano. I miss Ma a lot. ❀

Some of the hundreds of original sheet music I inherited from Ma; many pieces date back to the early 1900s.

Nunthing Ventured, Nunthing Gained

$\mathcal{M}$y fellow novices were silent with hands folded. Mother Superior hovered around us, floating like a spirit, checking whether we were kneeling perfectly straight, our heads bowed devoutly in prayer.

In Roman Catholic grade school, I learned from Sister Kathleen to fold my hands straight. Kneel straight. Genuflect straight. She'd slap my hands, knees or back with her long ruler when I didn't follow her strict posture guidelines. Palms held tightly together and fingers pointing toward heaven, I knelt ramrod straight.

At eight years old, I felt pretty and proud, walking down the center church aisle in my new lily-white dress, one of two new dresses I got as a child. Before receiving the Sacrament of Holy Communion, I had to go to my first confession and tell my sins to a priest, which petrified me because I didn't know what to say. Not wanting a soul to hear what I said, I went into the small dark booth, closed the door, knelt on the cushioned kneeler, and whispered through the small veiled opening, "Bless me Father, for I have sinned. I disobeyed my parents and talked back to my teacher. I told lies, but I'm not sure which things I said were lies." The priest said, "Now go and say three Hail Marys. May the Lord forgive you and be with you." I figured since my Penance only took about a minute to say that I must not be a big sinner because some other kids stayed in church praying longer.

When I received my First Communion I genuflected without wobbling or shaking and then stood and opened my mouth—not real wide open—just wide enough for the priest to gently lay a thin, round wafer on my tongue, which represented the body of Christ.

Sister Kathleen had also put the fear of God in us saying, "You must kneel on the floor before you get into bed—even if the floor is cold—and say the Act of Contrition." That was in case we died during the night, so that we'd have a better chance of getting into heaven right away. If not, we would go to Purgatory. I did not want to burn in a fire, ever. I did what she said.

We said ejaculations—which are short prayers, shorter than the Act of Contrition, like, "Jesus, Mary, Joseph, may I breathe forth my soul with you in peace." Ejaculatory prayers earned indulgences, like gold stars for good work, and granted full or partial reduction of time in Purgatory. I said thousands of ejaculations so I wouldn't go to Purgatory.

In eighth grade, I said to Gerry, "I got the calling to go to the convent." I didn't have a spiritual awakening. Nor did the Blessed Virgin Mary appear out of nowhere. Nothing like that happened at all. The nuns had drilled into us that in big families, at least one person should be a priest or a nun. I thought, *There are only three of us still at home who could possibly serve in the clergy, and neither Gerry nor Bobby are going to go, so I have to be the one.*

In his lighthearted way, Gerry said, "Deena, how could this be? We don't even have a phone."

Our two room schoolhouse for Grades 1-8

Gerry and I still keep in touch with several from our eighth grade class.

At fifteen, I joined the convent as an aspirant—a trainee nun—in The Franciscan Order of Perpetual Adoration in Prairie du Chien, Wisconsin. Some of us called it the Order of Perpetual Masturbation.

We attended school at St. Mary's Academy, about a mile from the all-boys Campion Jesuit High School. Living in the convent dorms near the school, I attended classes during the day at St. Mary's Academy with girls who were not studying to be nuns. The Academy was known for its superior education. Years later, I realized this excellent education helped me earn an academic scholarship for college and open doors in ways I'd only dreamed.

I swore full-fledged nuns had eyes in the back of their heads, because they inevitably caught me going out to take a walk alone and gave me the typical penance of praying in the chapel for half an hour, asking God forgiveness for disobeying.

Our regimented daily schedule required us to get up at 5:30 am, pray, then do early morning chores, like sectioning grapefruit, folding napkins, and squeezing oranges for juice before breakfast for the thirty of us, who lived in the convent.

The first years in the convent centered mostly on learning. In addition to attending high school and Latin classes, we were taught catechetical formation and formal nun etiquette like keeping our black tunic dresses wrinkle free and practicing correct posture, walking with shoulders straight, like we had a yardstick extending the length of our back.

I found the mandatory Golden Silence, from eight o'clock at night until six in the morning unbearable and broke this rule more than once. Consequently, I spent more time than most in the chapel doing penance for talking. During this quiet time, we were advised to listen closely to what God said to us. I couldn't seem to hear God talking to me at all.

The next step in the liturgical hierarchy was to be a novice, the time when we first wore a veil and took the temporary vows of poverty, chastity, and obedience. We also changed our birth names to convent names symbolizing a spiritual transformation and dying to the world we once knew. I became Sister Monica. But rather than feeling a closer connection to God, I felt spiritually adrift from Him, more out of sync, like I was in a distant land and didn't really exist.

Most of all, I couldn't grasp the thought of eventually taking confining vows that I had to follow my whole life, and having my hair sheared off.

Besides, I was attracted to a priest, who held services at the convent. He said to me, "You are beautiful and hugged and kissed me." I knew then I yearned for physical love because I didn't get or feel what spiritual love was supposed to feel like.

I'll never forget the time I took more than one helping of food at dinner. When Mother Superior spotted this with her laser eyes, she said, "Sister Monica, stand up right now and ask God's forgiveness. You are aware that gluttony is one of the seven deadly sins. Go to the chapel and hold your arms high above your head for half an hour like Jesus did when he died on the cross." Humiliated, still hungry and thin, I left the table with my eyes down, trying to hide my tears. *There must be other ways I could show my love for God than what I considered harsh and unfair punishment,* I thought. I never said a word. I decided I had to be strong as long as I could, liked I'd learned to do while growing up, even though I was miserable.

The routine was the same everyday, which drove me crazy. I wanted freedom to decide what to do and when, not be captive like a caged animal where most everyday is the same.

Only twice a year did the routine change. We were allowed to see an approved movie in the convent auditorium with the boys from Campion Jesuit School. I remember sitting near guys for the first time watching *A Raisin in the Sun* with Sidney Poitier. I sat in the last row right in front of the aspiring priests. Before the lights went off, I turned around and saw the boy behind looking straight at me. I looked right into his blue eyes. They twinkled like stars. He had black curly hair. He smiled so warmly. Several minutes into the movie, I put my right arm around the side of my chair to the back and the boy behind me held my hand. I got butterflies and was sad when the movie ended and he had to go back to the Jesuit residence. I never found out his name.

About a year later, Mother Superior and I agreed that I was not cut out for a life of poverty, chastity, and obedience. Overcome with relief, I cried with joy. I had been set free. I remember thinking, *I can't wait to wear shiny high heels.*

Sometimes I miss the Catholic Church, some of its traditions, the inspiring architecture, and the sense of community. When I do go to church now, I attend services of various religions. I value the foundation Catholicism has given me and that I learned to not only be a good person, but to do good for others as often as I can.

Spirituality for me is about love, compassion, acceptance, and peace no matter the religion. I believe we are all connected to a life force, which to me is God. ❀

Shiny high heels were not allowed in the convent.

Young and in Love

"**Y**ou're very attractive. You have striking features."

I loved compliments, especially nice ones like these from a man. I had never thought of myself as pretty, maybe because as a little girl, my mother and kids at school would say things like, "Your lips and mouth are too big for your face."

Larry swept me off my feet the first time I talked to him. His charisma, quick wit, and handsome features captivated me. He was a reporter for the *Rockford Morning Star*. I met him when he was covering an event at the healthcare facility where I worked in public relations. We dated, fell in love and in 1972, Thomas Larry Adcock and I married in an outdoor wedding in Madison, Wisconsin. We were both twenty-five when we moved to Minneapolis, a town where neither of us had ever lived, because of job opportunities available in both our fields.

Jessica with Anne, their dad, and me

Larry's six-year-old daughter, Anne, lived with her mother in Detroit, where Larry had previously worked at the *Detroit Free Press*. When Anne came to stay with us during the holidays and summer, we spent great times with her at libraries, museums, and art fairs. A happy and smart kid, Anne's face lit up whenever we talked about nature. She'd ask questions like, "What are falling stars?" "Do fish breathe in water?" "How does a caterpillar turn into a butterfly?"

Community activists, Larry and I rallied for causes, including the hazards of smoking after we both quit the habit. We prohibited smoking in our home, a novel practice in the seventies. Some guests remarked, "Oh, you're one of those!" We also supported local efforts to enact the first state Clean Indoor Act in 1975, a ground-breaking law back then. Larry voiced strong opposition in newspaper editorials and at public gatherings on "how smoking was not only bad for one's health, it was a disgusting and rude habit." Though the initial Clean Indoor Act still allowed smoking in public settings, it required creating no smoking areas. We hailed this as a good start to one day ban smoking. It took thirty-two more years before Minnesota enacted a statewide law to make public places smoke-free.

In our house in Minneapolis

As time went on, Larry became easily annoyed about the way I talked, especially when I used Midwestern slang.

"Yah, I'm gonna get gas fer the car."

"You wanna come with?"

"Ya betcha', I'll git the melk."

He'd say, "That is not proper English" and kept a list of some of my expressions on his desk. This upset me a lot. I thought, *How ironic that his friend, Garrison Keillor, creates fictional people who use this same slang on his radio talk show, which is getting rave reviews.*

Another time, during an evening dinner when we were entertaining his colleagues from the *St. Paul Pioneer Press,* I chimed in on the conversation and commented on a news event being discussed. Larry said, "You'll have to excuse Deena. She doesn't read the daily newspaper and isn't up on current news." What I said had apparently been inaccurate. I felt belittled. I wanted to crawl under the table. I said very little the rest of the evening to prevent other condescending remarks. Wanting to scream, I kept my mouth shut. More and more, little things I did or said irritated him. The tension mounted.

One day, when I came home from work, things were different. Pieces of furniture were gone. The house felt empty. Larry's spiral notebooks were missing from his desk and the bookshelves were bare. I ran upstairs to our bedroom and his closet was empty. I felt like throwing up. I called my baby-sitter to ask if Jessica, our three-year-old daughter, could stay with her. I cried through the night. I can't remember if he left a note. He had moved to New York, "the center of the universe," as he often referred to it.

The next day, tears rolling down my face, I told the Human Resources person at my company what had happened and that I could not focus on work. Very compassionate and kind, she hugged me and said, "This will all work out." She immediately scheduled a counseling appointment with a clinic that accepted my health insurance. That same day, I had a consultation with Laura, who became my therapist for years to come.

Calm, assured, and soft, Laura asked me how I felt.

"Rejected and all alone," I said. "I wonder how I could have kept our marriage together and made it work."

She listened and said something like, "Let's take one day at a time right now." After my first session, I felt a little better for a while. That feeling didn't last, especially when Jessica kept asking, "When is Papa coming home?"

I hugged her and said, "Not today, I know your papa loves you very much and cares a lot about you." I knew he had left me, not Jessica. If he could have taken Jessica, he would have. I didn't know the right thing to say to our precious little girl.

The nuns had instructed us that we marry once for life. My parents were married all their lives, not that they had a healthy marriage, but divorce was not an option for a devout Catholic like my mother. I detested any stigma of divorce. I felt everyone could see the word LOSER shining in neon letters on my forehead. Laura suggested that I refer to myself as single, rather than divorced, when asked. That felt a bit easier to say.

Laura taught me the skills I needed if I did marry again, like how to communicate in a constructive way. She explained that "rather than being a doormat and not discuss my feelings, it's best to express them in a nonconfrontational way." She taught me how to change things about myself rather than try to change others, which she emphasized, "is a futile endeavor. You can choose to be in control of your own happiness or be a victim. You can get rid of those useless tapes and feel good about yourself. Develop interests, pursue your passions, and help others. These are choices only you can make."

Tired of being sad, I made the choice to change and be happy. She suggested, "Help others and volunteer at a homeless shelter, your church, anywhere. Other people need you." I did as she advised and to this day feel fulfilled when I help make others' lives easier.

I moved forward. Grateful that my six-year marriage had given me a daughter and stepdaughter, I learned to know myself better, let go of the small stuff, and forgive myself as well as others.

Larry remarried in 1984. Jessica enjoyed flying to New York to be with him and her stepmother, Kim. When Jessica returned from her trips, she would say, "Papa and Kim make me laugh. Kim draws funny pictures with me. Papa reads with me and takes me to libraries." ❀

Special Delivery

My co-worker painted my pregnant belly.

*O*ne morning at my office, one of my business colleagues asked if she could draw a picture on my big belly. I said, "Sure." I read my mail while Marsha painted a wide-eyed funny face with my popped-out belly button as the nose. I thought her drawing was so unusual that I wanted to share it with the company management team, who were about to start their meeting in the boardroom. "Excuse me," I said, "Can I quickly show you something?" They said, "Yes. What is it?" I pulled up my top so they could see. They all burst out laughing with comments:

"What a great spot for that clown face!"

"You made my day."

"That's our Deena."

When the nurse handed my baby to me and said, "It's a girl!" I was overcome with awe. I couldn't take my eyes off her and said, "Thanks so much for my special delivery."

She had a round face with bright pink blotches. She weighed 8.2 pounds, a pound more than the average weight of a baby girl, but she seemed tiny to me. I kept checking her to make sure she had ten fingers, ten toes, two eyes, two ears, and one nose. I believed having all of ones' limbs and body parts made life easier.

I loved showing off my beautiful baby.

Larry and I named her Jessica, an uncommon name in 1975. We both liked the melodic sound of the name and its meaning, "God Beholds" or "God's Grace" from the Hebrew yishai, or gift. Jessica's paternal grandmother was Jewish.

When I got pregnant, I was living in Minneapolis, married for three years and working on a marketing team for a small, privately held distribution company. I wanted at least three kids. Larry knew I wanted to get pregnant and, at some point, we decided to have a baby. When I went to the doctor for a pregnancy test, I was elated the results were positive. At that time, no medical test had been invented to determine whether it was a boy or a girl. I wanted a girl, but more importantly, I wanted a healthy baby, regardless of gender.

During the first eight months of my pregnancy, I was a pitcher on a co-ed softball team. I took the liberty of eating more than my share of chocolate malts. If I ate a lot, I figured I would look pregnant sooner, and

dispel any notion that I was getting fat. I gained more than recommended, but achieved my goal of looking pregnant.

Jessica was lively...

I kept asking the doctor if I was having twins, hoping since I was a twin, myself that I might have twins. But there weren't two embryos. My doctor advised me to cut down on my calorie consumption. I cut out malts the last month because I did not want a fat baby. I also wanted my baby to be healthy and smart, and gave up all alcohol.

I remember Larry and I going to classes to learn how to breathe correctly during labor. The night before Jessica was born, the contractions started and got more frequent. Larry and I drove to the hospital and we did the breathing techniques we had practiced. The sharp pains became regular and they hurt. They were like bombs going off inside me. I screamed a lot. The nurses said I was disturbing others on the same floor and advised me to put a cloth over my mouth. I was finally given an epidural to ease the pain and calm me down.

After fourteen hours of labor, early in the morning on a cool fall day in November, Jessica was born. I don't recall if Larry was in the room. All I remember is I was worn to a frazzle.

I was happy when I was able to bring Jessica home, but not sure what to do first. Fortunately, my mother came to live with us for the first five months to help care for her. I nursed Jessica for six weeks before I went back to work.

During my lunch hour, I would drive home to nurse her. Our home was about ten minutes from my office. One day, in a heavy snowstorm in January, I slid off the icy road into a ditch. There were no cell phones then. I knew Jessica needed her milk. I used all my weight to push the car door as hard as I could with my feet so it would open and I could climb the snowy slope. I waved down the first car that came along and asked the driver for help. He drove me straight home. Jessica was upset and crying when I arrived. Larry came home from work and drove me back to my car, where a tow truck had pulled it out of the ditch.

...and precocious

Throughout her early years, I kept detailed notes in a baby book about Jessica's personality, likes and dislikes, and things she said.

Eleven months: Curious. Always looking inside bags, closets, drawers and cupboards. Says several words: ball, bye-bye, book, dog, mama. Loves to be with Anne when she visits. See sprigs of hair growing on her head. Walks alone without hanging on to anything.

Eighteen months: Has a vocabulary of about fifty-five words, including balloon, stink, bubble and snow. Pretends like she is reading the words when she looks through her books.

Two years: Carries around one of her stuffed animals most of day, especially her favorites: Leopold the Lion, Cookie Monster, Garfield and Big

Brown Bear. Likes to ride her tricycle, talks to Betsy our dog, loves to dance and sing. Extremely determined, and energetic. Answers questions in complete sentences: "Yes, I would prefer that kind of pudding."

Four years: Writes letters to her papa in New York. Had another birthday party with fourteen little kids and a round blue Cookie Monster cake. Constantly asks questions like, "How do our eyes see?" "Why can airplanes fly and people can't?" "Who made God?"

Creative and imaginative, she talks to her stuffed animals, saying things like:

"Wonder what you would look like if your fur was skin."

"There, I did it again. I let my imagination run wild on me."

To this day, her non-sequiturs still make me laugh:

"Betsy (our dog) thinks I'm a dog. I don't want to go outside to the bathroom. I like being a little girl and going to the bathroom inside."

"I like to swing in my night shirt because the air blows under my shirt."

One day, she came home from kindergarten and said, "Mom, I love you with my whole system. You know I mean my heart and all my bones and toes." And then, "Mom, are you aware that I stole the popsicles out of the fridge, took them to my room and ate them? After that I said bad words."

A very loquacious girl, Jessica kept herself occupied by explaining what she was doing to anyone who'd listen. She personified her animals, with which she had two-way conversations. I always wished I had more time with her when she was little, but I knew her grandma took good care of her when I was at the office.

The years flew by and Jessica grew up to become the independent, strong-willed, multi-talented person she is today. She has chosen to live in Jackson Hole, which she calls, "a slice of heaven," where she can enjoy her passions: scaling the Tetons, backcountry snowboarding, whitewater rafting, trail running, wake surfing, boating, and practicing yoga. She's traveled, lived, and worked in many different countries, making it her mission to interface with various indigenous cultures and learn from them.

I'm proud of her and what she's accomplished so far in your life: becoming bilingual, earning a master's degree, teaching Spanish and English, being a published writer, and giving back to her community as an advocate for the Latino population. I say to her, "I'm lucky to be your mother. Thanks for being a genuine and loving daughter. Remember to listen to others and always show compassion to those in need. I love you, with all my heart." 🏵

Christmas in Austin

The Slip Up

On a damp and overcast day, the heavy rain turned into hail and pounded against our upper floor apartment. Like the weather, the morning inside began noisily, with five-year-old Jessica crying, not wanting to go to school and leave her new Samoyed puppy. As I helped her get dressed and comb her hair, she asked me, "Mommy, could I stay home from school today? I don't want to leave Bojangles. He gets sad when we leave him alone all day." After some persuading, I convinced her that Bojangles would do just fine in his safe place, and promised I would make it a point to come home during my lunchtime to check on him and to let him outside.

While eating her cereal, she cried out, "Mommy, I spilled my orange juice on my drawing. I need it for show-and-tell at school." Without a minute to waste, I quickly pulled out the crayons and clean paper to help her do another drawing. The clock said seven-thirty, and I had to leave for day care to make it to the office twenty minutes away to present my strategic review at eight, the first person on the agenda.

I had spent a long time preparing and rehearsing my preparation. Our plans had to be thorough, factual and concise, outlining the opportunities, threats, risks, goals, strategies and projected annual return on investment. Having to be on top of my game, I must present myself in a professional manner, exuding confidence and total control, with no wiggle room for error. I felt the pressure more than usual. In the late eighties, many a career had been made and broken in this Honeywell conference room furnished with an oversized mahogany table and twelve extra-tall leather chairs.

Rehearsing my presentation one last time in my mind, while at the same time getting Jessica's backpack, lunch and homework, I grabbed my raincoat, put it on and rushed out the door. I left her at day care by 7:40, and I walked into the conference room at 7:53. With no time to spare, I took my

39

presentation out of my briefcase. Everyone was already in the room, most seated. I said to myself, *Be calm, cool and collected. Do not appear flustered. Be in control.*

Taking off my raincoat, I noticed several of the men staring at me and putting their hands over their mouths in seeming disbelief. Others just sat motionless, like they were frightened. I glanced down and what I saw mortified me: my white full-length slip and heels. My stomach dropped to the floor. I'm sure they noticed the shocked look on my face, flushed with humiliation. I had to think and act fast. Not the time to apologize and leave the room, I quickly decided that I must "get on with the show," just as Dad had always ordered us kids to do, no matter what happened.

Without fanfare, I put on my raincoat and said, "Now that I have your attention, let's begin." I delivered my marketing plan and had everyone's attention. I answered questions and supported my answers with facts and examples. When my time was up, I gathered my presentation and briefcase and walked out of the conference room directly to the elevator.

As fast as my legs could carry me, I dashed out of the elevator to my car, parked in the company garage, and drove home to put on my business suit. My emotions got the best of me. Alone, where no one could hear or see me, I sobbed loudly, thinking, *What have I done? How could I make such a career-limiting move? I'll lose my job because I forgot to put on my suit.*

Later in the day, my boss called me into his office. Terrified, I prepared myself for the worst. He stood up and motioned for me to sit on the leather armchair opposite him. I took a deep breath. He sat straight in his hi-back swivel chair behind his desk, looked directly at me and began; "We couldn't help but be startled during your review this morning." Not sure what to say, I waited for what seemed like several minutes. Probably only a few seconds passed before he continued, "You'll be pleased to know the group gave you a high rating. Your content, product knowledge, and grasp of the competition gave us a thorough picture of the market opportunity."

Sitting in front of him like a deer in headlights, I listened attentively. He proceeded to tell me my job performance was exemplary. "We admired how you handled what could have been awkward. You kept going forward and stayed on point." He got up from his chair, extended his hand and said, "I want to be the first to congratulate you, Deena. Great job!"

A tsunami of relief swept through me. Just a few minutes earlier, I thought my gaffe could end my career. On cloud nine and without acting too excited, I said, "Thank you, thank you," thinking, *Maybe this was good luck and my slip-up showed I could hold my own in precarious situations.* That night I poured myself a glass of wine, thanking God and the angels that I still had my job. ❀

In my office at Honeywell in the early 80s

Marrying a Family

"*I* am 39 years old!" Chuck said to our guests at his surprise birthday party. Few people believed him, which made the party even more fun. I had been able to surprise him by having his 40th party a year early.

The frosting on his birthday cake recreated the personals ad Chuck had placed in the newspaper *The Reader*: "Professional, attractive, secure, single parent, 5-feet-10, 155 pounds, enjoys outdoor activities, concerts, movies, computers, photography, fireplace talks, cuddling, etc. Seeking attractive female to share the above."

My reply letter said, "Friends describe me as a vibrant, slender business professional with a sense of humor, a yen for adventure and a free spirit. I too am a single parent with an eight-year-old daughter. My desire is to make you feel special and share with you my passion for good conversation, ideas, music, and jogging."

With no voicemail yet in the early eighties, when Chuck called, he always got my mother, who lived with us during the winter months taking care of Jessica. She talked to him a couple of times for about a half-hour each and said, "Chuck sounds like a very responsible young man. He is raising four kids alone and works a full-time job. He must get little sleep." Luckily, I viewed a ready-made family as a benefit, not baggage and I thought this would be good for Jessica, too.

The fourth time he called, I answered. He said there was something "appealing" about my response that kept him calling, even though I was never home. We learned we both worked at Honeywell; with over 100,000 employees worldwide, it would have been unusual had we met at the company. We talked for about a half-hour.

Because I wanted to see if he had a wife in the wings, we set up our first meeting the following Saturday for eight in the morning at Chuck's home.

When I arrived, kids kept pouring out and I asked jokingly, "Do you have any more hiding in the closets?"

On our first date, we had dinner with all the kids and my mother at my house. Chuck admitted that when he first read the personals he thought, "Isn't this pathetic that people have to place ads to meet someone? But I finally did because I didn't want to spend the rest of my life alone."

I said, "For me, after one marriage, I didn't want to rely again on romance and chemistry as the key factors for a lasting relationship. Plus, with a demanding career and raising a kid, I wanted a safe way to meet a potential partner that didn't take a lot of my time away from home."

Katie, Jessica, Heather, me, Chuck, Jenny, Jeff
Our blended family wedding in 1985.

We dated for over a year before Charles Walter Flammang and I married in September 1985 at St. Thomas Catholic Church in Minneapolis. (We were allowed to marry in the church since I had been granted an annulment from my marriage to Larry). Like something out of the movie *Sound of Music,* the wedding party consisted of Chuck's four kids, Heather, Jenny, Katie and Jeff—ages 12, 9, 8, 6, respectively—and my daughter, Jessica, almost 10. She drew big applause when she played the song, "Morning Has Broken" on her violin at the wedding service. A lively reception followed, complete with orchestra music, dinner, tributes, and a creative poem called "The Puzzle that Fits" delivered by a well-known local radio broadcaster, who enraptured the audience with his creatively written poem about our lives.

Both Honeywell employees—Chuck, a mechanical engineer and I, a business-to-business marketer—we worked during the day. In the evenings and on weekends, we spent our free time biking, rollerblading, and doing outdoor activities with the kids. We jumped for hours on our trampoline until I'd wet my pants and we'd all laugh. We'd go to movies and plays, get groceries, and shop for clothes. I loved when the kids cheered me on, "Come on! Faster! You can do it!" as I ran over the finish line in my 10K races. The kids attended the Sunday school classes I taught at St. Thomas Catholic Church and learned about God and the importance of treating all with respect. Before school, they reviewed their completed school assignments.

While I listened to the kids and packed their lunch bags, I'd insert individual positive notes into each one. They'd comment, "I can't wait to find out what my message says when I open up my bag." Examples of the messages included, "Happy thoughts mean happy days," and "I'm grateful for my family and friends."

Jessica still keeps this note in her wallet for inspiration.

When the kids had a no-school day, one of them would go on a business trip with me. A trip that stands out in my mind is the time Katie, then ten, went with me to New Orleans. During the daytime, she came with me to my meetings; later we'd walk through interesting sections of the city, like the French Quarter. Observant and taking in all the sights and sounds, she'd call home and say, "Dad, I think you would really like watching the ladies dancing on tables. Bourbon Street is noisy and there are so many people. I'm going to buy a whole box of beignets for you because they're yummy and look like little fried pillows dipped in powdered sugar."

Another time, Jeff, age eight, flew with me to New York. Little did I know he had a big surprise for me. When we arrived at our hotel across from Central Park, I said, "Jeff, New York is a big city and we have to stick together. Don't ever leave the hotel room without me or go out to the park alone." He said, "I promise and cross my heart," but I knew how much he loved exploring. While I was checking in, Jeff talked and talked to the hotel bellman. Jeff told him, "I love looking at the giant marshmallows floating in the sky when I'm on the plane. The buildings here are taller than in Minneapolis. I have to bend my head way back to see the top of them."

The following morning while I was in the shower, Jeff disappeared. Panicked, I called the bellman. He had not seen Jeff and called another hotel employee to run across the street to the park and look for him. Sure enough, there was Jeff, sitting on a little rock next to a pond with a frog in his hand. Relieved and not mincing words, I explained to Jeff that he must stay with me because anything could happen to him—and that the next time we needed to go to the park together.

Like many baby boomers with dual incomes, Chuck and I gave more to our kids than we had as children. We bought them brand name clothes—Ralph Lauren, Esprit, and Guess—to fit in with the other kids in the neighborhood. The acronym for our city, Edina—Every Day I Need Attention—said it all. For Christmas, each kid received a new Mac computer and software. At that point, I was working for Apple and, luckily, had an Apple discount. The kids spent a week in the summer camp of their choice, be it horse camp, space camp, or nature camp. All seven of us went on vacation to the Cayman Islands.

One of the most memorable vacations was a road trip to Disney World in Florida. Chuck and I drove non-stop for thirty-two hours in our station wagon while the five kids slept in the back of the car. In the middle of the night, we'd hear, "She's kicking me!" Then another one, "Whew, somebody farted!" When awake, the kids played different games we divvied up every four hours. When bored, we'd tell jokes or count the number of Minnesota license plates, write in journals, and sing songs. I remember we sang, "I Just Called To Say I Love You" over and over again. I said to the kids over and over again, "I love you." They would say the same.

Amid all the fun with the kids, Chuck and I squeezed in a social life and played walleyball—a combination of handball, tennis, and volleyball—with a close group of friends as often as we could. Running, sliding, diving for the rubber ball, we'd hit it hard off the walls and over the net in a racquetball court for hours until, exhausted, we called time out. We'd finish the night

Left to right: Heather, Katie, Jenny, Chuck, me, Jessica, and Jeff

eating a homemade dinner at one of the couples' homes, laughing, talking, partying, and playing charades.

From the outside, our lives probably looked nothing out of the ordinary. I tried to make things look effortless and masked the heartaches and strain Chuck and I dealt with. No one knew about the series of legal affidavits, at least nineteen, filed on us by Chuck's ex-wife, who was in a psychiatric hospital on and off over the years. I remember that the court affidavits were delivered on holidays or birthdays. Chuck and I handled these stressful times in our own way. He would vent and retreat to his room, slam the door, and work on his computer for hours. I would do something with the kids to distract myself, wondering if the madness would ever stop. I thought, *Maybe I'm the crazy one for staying and keeping this family together. Maybe I should just leave.*

Chuck and I were required by law to appear in family court and respond to the false accusations in order to keep the kids. To my amazement, I learned that in the State of Minnesota, a biological mother, no matter what her state of mind, could file affidavits alleging anything. One allegation said Chuck made the kids take off their clothes and run around naked on the boat. And there were others.

46

I was stressed to the max—working full time, raising the family, and dealing with court-imposed counseling sessions—with my nose to the grindstone most of the time. This took a toll on me. I rationalized that since I chose to marry a family, it was my duty to stay and raise the kids, so I did. I'd say, "When the grand piano is no longer here, it means I've left." Playing the piano calmed me and helped me escape to a happier place.

With the kids grown and out of the house, I decided to go back to counseling to figure out my life. The connection Chuck and I had at one time no longer existed. Our marriage had been more about the kids than our relationship. We'd shared many good times together and I loved the kids with all my heart; still do and always will. But, I knew that to be a good person to others meant I had to start taking care of myself.

Coincidentally, at the same time, Gartner, an information technology (IT) research company in Stamford, Connecticut, acquired J3 Learning, an IT training company where I was Marketing VP. The acquisition required the management team stay on with Gartner for a minimum of two years. Since we could telecommute from wherever we lived, this was my chance to start a new life in a new town where I knew no one.

In 1996, my grand piano was loaded on a truck and I moved to Austin, Texas, whose city slogan "Keep Austin Weird" exemplifies the appeal of the place I soon would call home.   🕸

Small Town Funeral

"If you don't go to other people's funerals, don't expect them to come to yours," Ma often said. I laughed because this didn't make any sense to me.

No matter who died in and around our small Midwestern town, whether Ma knew them or not, she went to their funerals and insisted several of us kids go with her. We complied, bellyaching and complaining during the mile ride up to St. Anthony's Catholic Church in Germantown. I'd say, "Why do I have to go to funerals for people I don't even know?"

My non-religious dad never came into church, but would drive us there since Ma didn't drive. He'd wait for us in the car or at one of the local bars until the service ended.

Walking quietly to a front-row pew, we could easily see the deceased in the open casket, perched above the top step right in front of the church altar. I'd cringe when I looked at the corpse, and my stomach would get queasy seeing the head of the deceased propped up on a silky pillow in the casket, as if on exhibit in a showroom. The mortician made the dead look so alive that often I thought they were just sleeping and would suddenly open their eyes, sit up, and look at me.

On the wall behind the casket, Jesus' body hung on a gigantic wooden cross: blood dripped from his heart, hands, feet, and down his face, and a huge crown of thorns pierced his head. I wondered who decided to build this king-size cross depicting such a gory scene instead of something beautiful and inspiring, like a picture of Jesus performing the miracle of loaves and fishes. That despondent image of Jesus is etched forever in my mind, having looked at it thousands of times: before school days each morning, Sundays, holy days, weddings, funerals, and while saying penance after confession.

When Ma died at 81, a nearby radio station, WRDB in Reedsburg, broadcast this announcement: "Hilda Compton of Cazenovia passed away the morning of February 4, 1994. Eight children, twenty grandchildren, several great grandchildren, and many relatives survive her. She is one of a family of twelve and is also survived by several brothers, sisters, and their children. Her husband, Arthur Morton Compton, two sisters, a brother and parents, John and Catherine Rockweiler, preceded her in death."

I thought few people would come to Ma's funeral because so many of her friends and relatives from our town in Cazenovia, Wisconsin, population only 325, had already died. To my surprise, a couple hundred people ventured out to bid her farewell on one of the most frigid days in February, the temperature at minus 40, with the wind chill. Packed like sardines in the church, my nieces, nephews, uncles, aunts, cousins, friends, neighbors, and strangers crammed into the pews and stood side-by-side in the aisles. Mourners of all ages came in their down winter coats with furry collars, long wool scarves wrapped around their necks, thick mittens, fleeced-lined boots, including a blind lady, pushed by her husband in a wheelchair. The crowded church didn't seem large enough to hold Ma's huge heart and universal spirit.

Like the Catholic funerals I remember attending as a child, Ma's funeral service was also somber. People sobbed as my 17-year-old daughter, Jessica gave this heartfelt eulogy.

> *"Grandma*, I will forever cherish all my times with you in your kitchen: cutting out edges of envelopes and newspapers to use for making paper snowflakes, reading your mountains of mail and birthday cards, and saving all the return addresses, while listening to your stories in the summer nights with the Wisconsin crickets chirping on the porch.
>
> You taught me to love winter, the snow, music, and words. I remember you always putting on your 'rubbers' over your tan Dr. Scholl's to go outside in the cold Minnesota winters when you came to live with us, and how we would sing together while you played the piano for hours and hours until my mom came home from her long work days and business trips. You took away my loneliness with your music and your shining face, singing lines to 'I Don't Want to Play in Your Yard' and my favorite, 'Beautiful Ohio.' The spittle that shot from your dentures while you sang never even bothered me."

Tears streaming down her face, Jessica continued. "I enjoyed my times with you, cutting out coupons into the wee hours of the evening, sleeping with you in your lumpy bed, the mattress holes stuffed with nylons, and the room heaped with stacks of age-old newspapers you just couldn't throw away. We would pick raspberries until my fingers bled from the fuzzy thorns, and we'd frost the beautiful angel food cakes you made for birthdays—the blue icing always my favorite—and then stick the numbered candles on top for the photographs you'd take. I loved making lists with you in the dark of night: grocery lists, thank-you card lists, birthday lists. You kept me busy so I wouldn't miss my mother. I spent so much time alone with you, growing up an only child, until my mom remarried. Grandma, I'll treasure those days all my life.

Sitting next to me, you taught me the secrets of life and gave me purpose. I still use every scrap of paper, make lists, read the paper daily, and make a ritual out of putting on my boots to go outside in the snow.

Mostly, I loved praying with you. We prayed to St. Jude, the Virgin Mary, the Holy Ghost and more. I didn't know who any of these figures really were, but I loved the sound of the words, the recitation and the ritual. You taught me to have faith in something bigger than myself and showed me what love is. You taught me to show others the companionship and love you showed me. Grandma—so patient, so kind, so giving—I love you."

Ma and Jessica celebrating with a birthday cake

We finished the service singing hymns, including, "Amazing Grace," "How Great Though Art," and "You Are Mine." I wondered why songs were mostly sad at Catholic funerals. I wished we could have sung one of the comforting songs Ma used to sing, like "The Angels are Lighting God's Little Candles," because then I could imagine when I looked up at the stars, it was her twinkling in them.

Six male cousins carried Ma's casket from the hearse through the crunching snow to her burial site next to Dad in the Cazenovia cemetery. They carefully set it down on the boards above the place where the hole would be dug once the freeze lifted. Thinking of her being left out in the cold made me shiver. I knew how much she disliked the biting Wisconsin winters. Her clapboard house had no insulation and she'd say, "It's so cold, I bet hell is freezing over. The chill shoots directly through me and to my bones."

If only I could hook up a small heater to set near her casket to keep her warm, I thought. Sprinkling her casket with holy water, the priest said the final prayer: "May her soul and the souls of all the faithful departed through the mercy of God rest in peace." Hollow inside, my tears froze solid on my face as the fierce wind blew and heavy snow beat down. I kissed the casket lightly. I didn't want my lips to get stuck. Others touched her casket and said their goodbyes as the rest of the crowd rushed to their cars to get warm.

After the burial, we drove back to Germantown to the funeral reception, organized and catered by the Catholic Church Women's Guild volunteers, who covered the tables with homemade foods from ham, stew, casserole dishes, mashed potatoes and breads, to puddings, cakes, pies, and home-made ice cream.

I socialized with many people who had gathered together in memory of Ma. More came to the reception than the funeral, mostly due to the frigid weather. During her life, I knew how much people loved her, but hearing person after person tell me how they felt about her made me feel blessed that this amazing person was my mother.

Jeanne, a tall lady who lived about a mile down the road from Ma, hugged me and said, "Hilda was one of the kindest, most generous, and thoughtful ladies I've ever known. She never complained about her difficult life, but instead found good in the smallest of things, like the currants and raspberries she grew and made into jam."

Just then, a stout elderly woman tapped me on the shoulder, smiled and said, "Whenever I visited Hilda or she came over, she would bring me

51

her special homemade cinnamon rolls or chicken noodle soup, and we'd talk for hours."

Ma's young neighbor came over to me and said, "Your mother was like a grandma and best friend. Whenever I stopped over, she would offer me food, ask me how I was doing and made me feel like she had all the time in the world for me. I'll really miss having her next door."

Another man, whom I recognized, but whose name I couldn't remember, walked slowly toward me, leaning on his cane, and said. "You're one of the twins, right? I want you to know Hilda meant the world to me. She listened to my problems and spent time with me. I'll remember her as our angel here on earth. She gave what she could and had so little herself. "

I said, "Thanks for your kind words. I love her and will miss her."

I knew then, after attending several sad funerals, that I would plan mine in advance. I would request lively, upbeat music with people singing, laughing, and celebrating with stemmed wine glasses held up in unison, making a toast to all the good times we'd had. There would be pictures of my life with family and friends displayed on big screens, so people could see them from any spot in the room with tall ceilings. Everyone would be given a small fortune cookie or balloon, with a surprise message from me tucked inside.

Years later I understood what Ma meant when she said, "If you don't go to other people's funerals, don't expect them to come to yours." This was her way of telling us to make a difference in the lives of others by showing up at funerals and giving comfort to the people left behind. These past couple of years, I've followed her example and paid last respects to twenty-one people, most from my advanced cancer group, which I've been a member since being diagnosed with Stage IV cancer.

As Ma often said, "The only permanent thing in life is change. Since none of us are going to get out of here alive, be good to others while you are still here." ❊

The Judge's Verdict

The house at 6617 Southdale Road in Edina, MN

$\mathcal{A}$ll hell broke loose when we decided to sell our house in the city of Edina, just southwest of downtown Minneapolis. For years, Chuck and I had shared the spacious four-level split house with our blended family and an elderly unrelated live-in helper, whom the kids called 'Grandpa'—eight of us in all.

Linda, our real estate agent met with us and said, "Your house is sure to get offers right away because it's in a high-demand area and has amenities people want: six spacious bedrooms, three baths, open living spaces, and large rooms, including the kitchen, dining and living areas."

She shared the description of our home with others in her real estate company, and one of her colleagues, Rena, called A Better Chance Foundation

(ABC) to see if they would be interested. Soon after, ABC board president made the first offer on our property. A housemother, housefather, and seven female scholars would live in our home and attend Edina High to receive a top-notch education.

Once we accepted the offer, ABC hung flyers on residents' doors to let them know ABC planned to purchase our house for house parents and high-achieving girls from underprivileged areas across the nation, so the young women could have an academic opportunity, not accessible to them in their neighborhoods. ABC held an open house, which was attended by the Lieutenant Governor, the Mayor of Edina, and members of the Viking Football team to meet and talk with the prospective residents and neighbors. We believed our almost all-white suburb of 35,000 people would welcome diversity and did not anticipate what was about to happen.

Gossip in the neighborhood about the potential sale of our home to the ABC had circulated like wildfire and morphed into absurdity. Some comments heard from Edina residents:

"We have a safe community. Imagine what could happen if people like them moved in."

"There will be increased traffic, noise, and underage drinking."

"I hate to think of what trouble they will cause."

"Did you hear that a crack house will be in our neighborhood?"

Some 550 Edina residents, including best friends on the same block signed a petition calling for a review and revision by the City Council of the zoning codes governing single-family residential housing. In part, the petition read, "We appreciate the availability of programs such as shelters for battered women . . . group homes for the mentally disabled, and hospitals for the elderly or terminally ill. However, we also believe it is prudent for Edina's Zoning Codes to restrict the location, proximity and obligations of residential programs."

When the petition came before the Edina City Council, several meetings followed with "heated debate from a parade of speakers and letter-writers championing either the zoning review or the ABC program," according to an October 1993 article in the *Edina Sun Current*. In mid-November, the City Council decided not to review the city ordinances because they had been codified a year earlier.

A report from the local police department circulated with several calls made from residents since the impending sale, claiming that there were loud

54

parties and cars parked in the driveway and in front of our Southdale house. Each time the police knocked at our door, we invited them in. Once, they saw Chuck and me playing charades and laughing with friends. Another time, the police were called, our kids were watching videos with friends in the recreation room on the lower level, drinking soda, and eating popcorn. They told the kids to keep the noise down as a neighbor had complained. We couldn't help but think we were being harassed.

Unfortunately, the drama did not end.

Ironically, Chuck selected a moving company, called ABC Transfer from six estimates he'd received. On moving day, unbeknownst to us, the truck that parked in our driveway, had ABC emblazoned in blue bold letters on a white background on its sides. The movers started loading the truck. When some residents saw the truck, they apparently thought ABC was moving in. Didn't anyone notice that belongings were being loaded onto the truck, not out of the truck?

This prompted a group of residents to take further action to prevent the sale of a "single-family" home on Southdale Road to ABC, and a few days later, after we had moved out, the issue was escalated to the Hennepin County District Court, who in turn, issued a restraining order on Chuck and me, the city of Edina, and ABC until the matter could be decided by the Court.

We delved into our meager savings and hired an attorney to defend what we believed to be morally right. Ethnicity was the only difference between the ABC family and us; neither fit the Census Bureau's traditional definition of a family, termed "a group of two people or more (one of whom is the householder) related by birth, marriage, or adoption and residing together." In our viewpoint, the lawsuit cloaked underlying motivations to prevent the sale to ABC.

Almost four months after ABC's offer, District Judge Debra Hedlund ruled ABC's proposed use of the property complied with Edina zoning ordinances. *The Minneapolis Tribune* stated, "ABC's residence is for a functional family or single-housekeeping unit," according to Judge Hedlund, who could not 'define a family,' which is ever-changing. She continued, "Further the Flammangs are entitled to recover attorney's fees and costs from the plaintiffs who made a frivolous and costly claim."

The court issued a Sheriff's Writ of Execution, which meant the fees we had paid to represent ourselves, could be taken from any of the petitioners' bank accounts. Our attorney became a detective. Having no clue which banks the petitioners used, he searched several banks until all our legal fees could be recovered. The owner of the account asked the other plaintiffs to help him pay the legal fees, but not all contributed, causing a rift among the group.

Star Tribune

SATURDAY/November 13/1993   N E W S P A P E R   O F   T H E   T W I N   C I T I E S

ABC program's Edina home runs into Z – zoning

By Wayne Washington
Staff Writer

There is no hateful edge or venom in Greg Carlin's voice.

In even, measured tones, the 8½-year Edina resident spells out the problem as hundreds of others

there see it: A Better Chance Foundation, which takes inner-city students from across the country and places them in suburban schools to give them "a better chance" for a top-notch education, simply should not be allowed to buy a home in a residential section of Edina to house its students.

It's all about zoning, Carlin said. It has nothing to do with the fact that these are minority, inner-city kids, he said.

Hearing that argument, Gardner Gay, ABC's president, offers a wry smile and points out that zoning was the reason some residents used

to oppose ABC when it opened its first house for students in Edina in 1969. But that's about all Gay would say about ABC's detractors.

He's a product of the program. Having the unflinching support of

Home continued on page 10A

Our case was in the papers often.

While all this was happening, local TV news crews parked in the street outside our house and reported on the court case about the impending sale of the house on Southdale Road. We were not interviewed. We felt like pariahs in Edina. Friends had turned against us as well as some residents we didn't even know. Our only supporters included our attorney, real estate agent, and ABC president, who said to us, "ABC supports any decision you make. If you decide not to sell your house to our organization, we understand. It is not our intent to cause you any loss."

About a year after ABC had lived in the house, the same TV stations broadcast interviews with local residents touting the culturally diversity in Edina, citing the annual increase in the integration numbers, racial tolerance, and the graduation rate of ABC students. And Edina was recognized as one of the top US multicultural communities providing youth of any ethnicity with a variety of community service and leadership programs.

Since that time, twenty-two years ago, ABC girls have called our former house their home. Chuck and I believe that standing up for what we knew to be legally and morally right served as an impetus for this change. ❁

The Apple of my Eye

I picked a salmon hors d'oeuvre from a table overflowing with tempting appetizers, each platter, a work of art. The salmon had all my favorite toppings: capers, red onions, dill sauce, and lemon. I heard a familiar voice, "Deena, Deena, is that you? It's me, Bill." I turned around to see a huge smile on the face of my former marketing team member. He graciously took my plate, set it on the table, and gave me a warm hug. He pulled out my chair and we sat down to chat and recall our lively days at Apple.

Bill and I, along with fifty other former Apple employees, were at the Minnesota Valley Country Club to celebrate the 30th birthday of the Apple Macintosh (Mac) in March 2014. I reconnected with my colleagues, many of whom I hadn't seen since leaving Apple twenty-two years before.

I had flown from Austin to Minneapolis early the same morning and met my good friend, Mary, who had flown from Chicago, at the airport. We had worked together at Apple, she in sales, and I in marketing. We rented a car and drove to the celebration.

Just like past events at Apple, a professional photographer took scads of photos. Part of the evening's program included

Such a happy reunion with my former Apple colleague Bill

FaceTime with hundreds more employees gathered at the party in Cupertino's Apple headquarters. Seeing and hearing from several people who were still with the company after so many years made me instantly feel that same spirit and camaraderie I had when at Apple.

We raved about the days in the eighties and early nineties when we worked in Apple's cutting-edge culture. We had an evangelistic zeal to "change the world," and visualized computers on everyone's desktop. Steve Jobs' creation of a cult-like, free-spirited, risk-taking culture—which I wore like a badge—permeated Apple as if it were American folklore. Enthusiastic and committed, I, like others, pulled all-nighters when necessary. Rewards for our achievements came in the form of recognition and welcome compensation benefits.

My close friend Mary and me celebrating our years at Apple.

Vastly different from Honeywell, Apple did not have conventional protocols and hierarchical management. Even business cards at Honeywell required approval and a lengthy execution process. At Apple, the turn-around time on most processes was fast, and we had the liberty to be creative with our business cards. Some of my coworkers suggested "Goddess of Marketing" would be a catchy title on my card; indeed it was, sparking some lively discussions and people bowing down, pretending I was a Greek goddess. To underplay the words somewhat, I decided 'goddess of marketing' should be in lower case letters on my card.

I'll never forget my very first day at Apple, seeing my own Mac sitting on my desk. I felt I had won the lottery as I caressed the Mac keyboard for the first time. I couldn't wait to learn how to use it. For the previous ten years at Honeywell, I had used dumb terminals linked to a huge mainframe stored in a cold room.

First, I asked our tech guy Paul, "Where do I find my mail." He replied, "On your computer." I looked on all four sides of the monitor and the CPU box. "I can't see the mailbox anywhere," I said aloud. He heard me, turned on the computer, clicked the mail icon and said,

"Here's your mail."

"Doesn't Apple get paper mail like other companies?"

"Noooooo, everything is electronic here."

With an inner drive to achieve, I bloomed in Apple's dynamic culture. I pushed my imagination to the max. Sometimes, I would leave the office to drive my kids to their after-school events because I found that taking a little break and listening to the things they said about their day stimulated my imagination. I'd go back to my office rejuvenated. At lunchtime, to clear my mind for new ideas, I would jog on the path near our office. When my boss, Tom, looked out his window, he'd comment to others, "There's Deena running to get her creative juices going. Wonder what she will think of next. Knowing her, whatever she comes up with will be original."

In the early nineties, we launched the wickedly fast Mac IIfx, code-named the "Stealth and Blackbird." We organized an extravagant event for the Minnesota region and offered a free Mac in a raffle, and goodie bags with brochures and a special Mac application loaded on a CD. Since Apple was not yet a household word, we were surprised that more than twelve hundred people showed, twice what we estimated. We packed as many chairs as possible in the ballroom. The audience screamed and pounded the floor with excitement when the Mac was unveiled and we were all ecstatic that orders for our latest model exceeded sales projections.

I am proud of what I accomplished at Apple. I had a sense of purpose. Years later, I realized I had been part of a time of exciting growth in a revolutionary company.

Sitting around the table with my former colleagues, we reminisced, laughed, and agreed our years at Apple were among the best in our careers. The 1990 Apple campaign slogan said it all—"the power to be your best." ✿

Sharing stories from the good old days

The Well-Executed Plan

*T*he bright moon cast a shadow on the center campus colonnade. Leaning against the columns, Brent, a classmate, asked me, "What brought you to Stanford?"

"I've wanted to come here for years, but didn't have the money or time. When my CEO gave me the choice of a graduate business program or a cash bonus, I jumped at the opportunity and applied here because I wanted to attend a university renowned for cultivating entrepreneurship."

I asked, "And what made you decide to select Stanford?"

"I wanted to learn the rules of the road about business and apply them to a leadership role in my company," he said. "I know a lot about what to do as an institutional and commercial design architect, but need to know what it takes, business-wise, to lead a company. Originally I was going to Harvard, but due to a work conflict, I had to change dates and feel lucky to get into Stanford."

Something about Brent made me blurt out, "I also wanted to take this time away from a town I've been part of for twenty-four years and figure out a way to start a new life. Maybe you can give me some advice, from a man's perspective, on how to do this. I've moved out a couple of times and then moved back in with my husband. I want to be happy and move forward in my life."

I thought, *What do I have to lose? Besides, I'll never see him again after the program ends.*

Brent said, "Let me think about it. We can talk later. Let's get to our evening class right now."

We met at the Stanford Graduate School of Business. Sixty people—only four women—had been selected from applicants throughout the world to attend the intense summer program for growing small businesses. Half our classmates were from the US and the other half from various countries.

All dressed up

Brent, in his mid-40s, with a chiseled-like Roman face, and salt and pepper hair, looked and acted like an English gentlemen. He always pulled out my chair and waited till I sat down before he did. We sat next to each other whenever we could—in classes, at meal times, and in breakout sessions. We studied and exercised together. We went golfing, dancing, and sightseeing with our classmates. We talked about our lives and what we were learning.

Later, when the program ended, Brent said, "I believe I have an answer to your question. I think you and I should be together. What do you think?"

Surprised and happy at the same time, I said, "Wow. I know we relate on many levels. I feel our powerful connection. You're easy to talk to. We have many similar interests. How do we make this happen when you live in Dallas and I live in Minneapolis?"

He said, "Let's apply one of the key things we've learned here at Stanford—make a plan and execute it—even if we have to modify parts. Let's write it together. We can do it."

Brent had learned as much as he could about me in a short time: the good, the bad, warts and all. I'd bombarded him with questions, learning as much as I could about him before we left Stanford.

Then, we communicated by phone and followed each step of our four-step plan.

1) I wanted each of us to meet at least three single or married friends of the other and ask any question we wanted.

2) Together we would select a town in which we both wanted to live.

3) I needed to finalize my divorce.

4) Brent had to resign from the architectural firm where he was a partner. This was a tough decision as he had worked at the firm for twenty-four years, and was being considered for a major leadership role.

We flew to each other's hometowns and spent several hours talking with friends, both together and alone. I quickly realized that Brent was a well-connected, highly admired architect, and ingrained in the city. His friends would make comments like, "Brent has done so much for this city. We call him Mr. Dallas." They would look at Brent and ask, "How can you possibly move away from us? We need you here." One of his friends commented, "Maybe Brent is going through a mid-life crisis."

When Brent met my friends, he was his low-key self. Not a person to talk about himself or his accomplishments, he'd turn the conversation off himself and find out more about the person to whom he was talking, listening attentively to what each said. When he talked to them one-on-one, he told me, they said, "They'll miss you, but want you to be happy and be sure I treat you well."

One of my friends said, "Deena is the salt of the earth. She's a hard worker, involved in so many community circles, and loves to laugh. I'm her best friend and know her inside and out. Everyone thinks they are her best friend, but just so you know, I am."

A romantic moment

Another friend commented, "You probably noticed already how determined and energetic Deena is. She never stops. I hope you can help her slow down some."

From the three cities on our list, we chose Austin over San Diego and Atlanta because it met all our key criteria: university town, high-tech industries, and a warm climate, with the advantage of rolling hills like in Wisconsin where I grew up.

After living together for over a year and completing our plan, Brent wanted to get married. Though we shared an idyllic life, I thought long and hard about marrying again. I said. "I'm not sure this is a good idea for me yet. I don't want to mess up the best relationship I've had in my life, and based on my past history of two marriages, I'm afraid that I could. If we get married, we must stay married until one of us dies." We discussed my qualms and talked often about how things were going between us. In my gut, I knew Brent believed in me, our lasting love, and that we were meant to live the rest of our lives together.

In early 1998, I accepted his proposal and married Brent Eugene Byers in the Austin Travis County Courthouse. Since we'd both had previous wedding ceremonies, we decided on a low-key service with only two witnesses. Brent jokingly said, "I'm bolting your grand piano to the floor. You are never leaving. Instead of any more spouses, let's renovate houses."

I said, "That's a fabulous plan. This is my final marriage. I'm tired of spending money on counseling and changing my last name."

A year later, we attended my former husband's wedding in Minneapolis, a very festive and fun event.

To keep our marriage commitment front and center in our lives, Brent and I have made or purchased simple wedding rings in the countries where we've traveled throughout South America, North America, Africa, Asia and Europe. We especially treasure the rings we made deep in the rainforest of the Amazon and have worn often over the years. We each cut out the inside of an African chonta seed and kept the roundish outer shell, sanding the shell with varying grits of sandpaper until the color changed from an uneven light brown to a smooth dark brown, and fit the size of our fingers.

One of the happiest surprises in my marriage was the day Brent brought home a multicolored wooden carousel horse from a vintage fifties carousel. He knew I loved riding the carousel as a child and looked and looked for years before he found one in a local antique shop. After doing thorough research, Brent tediously restored the horse to its original colors. He cleaned, fixed, and painted the faded areas with special paints.

I named the horse Harmony. He lives in our kitchen, suspended from the high ceiling, overlooking daily life, special events and parties. Harmony's playful smile warmly welcomes everyone into our home filled with love, laughter, cheer, and lots of good times. ❀

Hanging out with Harmony at one of my holiday parties

Catalog Pages

I was the only woman among four male colleagues on our Newgistics' management team attending a high-level meeting with Sears executives on the top floor of their mammoth headquarters in Chicago. I wore my charcoal Dana Buckman suit with a red and black patterned scarf, feeling confident; however, the massive conference room intimidated me.

In early 2000, the Sears building was the tallest skyscraper in the world.

The only thing visible when I looked out the gigantic floor-to-ceiling windows were big floating clouds, making me feel suspended in space and time, ungrounded in a way.

I tried to stay focused on what I was saying. But while I was talking, I had a déjà vu moment that I could not put out of my mind. I saw those times, as a child, using the Sears catalogues for toilet paper in our outhouse. I had this

from the corporate website

strong, unexpected urge to say, *Wonder what you'd do if you knew I had to use Sears' catalog pages for toilet paper? You wouldn't believe how much I hated wiping my butt with slippery and nonabsorbent catalogs. They made my ass so sore my mother had to put salve on it. Why didn't you make your pages more soft and supple?*

The words almost shot out of my mouth. I bit my tongue, managed to stifle my overwhelming impulse and blocked out my thoughts.

It would have been totally inappropriate and potentially career limiting. I had worked for years in tech companies and certainly did not want to make a bizarre faux pas in this important meeting. Fortunately, everything went smoothly and Sears became one of our main customers.

Flying back home to Austin, I found myself reflecting on growing up with an outdoor biffy and how grateful I was for indoor plumbing with soft toilet paper. ❀

Trying not to mention my previous experiences with Sears catalogs.

67

The First Time

*B*rent felt the lump and pestered me for two months to go to the doctor. I never felt it. I thought, *If there is one in my breast, I won't give it any energy and it will go away.*

To appease Brent, I finally made an appointment with my gynecologist, Dr. Roberta Braun, who felt my breast and said, "There is some distortion at the left mid breast, upper outer quadrant. I'll order a sonogram." The next day I had the noninvasive medical procedure and the sonogram report stated, "Shows an irregular mass corresponding to a palpable lump. Suspicious. Needle biopsy recommended."

Dr. Braun sent us to our primary physician, Dr. Ron Byrd, who discussed the situation with us and called Dr. Robert Marcus, a surgeon he thought highly of, to perform the biopsy the next day. At this point, I was not concerned because I felt fine and firmly believed the biopsy would show the tumor was benign. Instead, the results stated, "a cancerous tumor." I started to get scared, but still believed that it could be taken out and all would be fine.

We met again with Dr. Byrd and Dr. Marcus and decided to take immediate action to get this taken care of and behind us. Two days later, Dr. Marcus cut out the cancerous tumor, which was about four centimeters across, and he also cut out fifteen of the lymph nodes in my armpit, where the cancer had spread. He said, "I cut out the maximum possible and think I got it all. The cancer was very close to your chest wall, which is probably why the mammograms didn't detect it."

In our follow-up meeting with Dr. Byrd, he said we needed to see an oncologist to discuss a treatment plan. He highly recommended Dr. Thomas Tucker and made an appointment for us two days later. For the first time, I felt anxious because everything was moving so fast and I was holding down a demanding job as VP of Marketing for the World Congress on Information

Technology. Nor did I have the time to read all the accolades posted on the Internet about Dr. Tucker.

A middle-aged man of medium stature, raised brows with round, gold, wire-rimmed glasses, entered the exam room, greeted us and asked how we were doing. After the kind exchange, Dr. Tucker, soft-spoken, yet direct, said, "I would like to first address your CT scan." Without beating around the bush, he said, "You have what is known as HER2/neu, Stage III Breast Cancer. The good news is that Stage III is treatable and potentially curable, whereas Stage IV is treatable, but not curable."

He said some more stuff that made little sense to me. I was in a fog, baffled and confused. Brent listened attentively and asked questions. I was in shock.

After regaining my senses, I discussed the diagnosis with Brent and did a lot of research. Simply put, my breast cancer type is Triple Positive, although no type is simple. In other words, my body was sensitive to the naturally occurring female hormones–estrogen and progesterone–and also overproducing the HER2 protein.

I thought, *How could this happen to me? I jogged daily, ate the right foods, seldom sick with even a cold, and felt on top of the world. No. The doctor is talking about someone else, not about me.* I hit a low point in my life. Brent was worried and felt like his foundation was crumbling. He's a fixer and wanted to fix something, but he couldn't fix this.

Within days we made another appointment with our surgeon, Dr. Robert Markus. It was time to have a port-a-cath implanted under my skin, on the upper right side of my chest, for the chemo treatments.

Before chemo, I decided to take control of something within my power and instead of waiting until my hair fell out, I had a shaving party with friends. I asked my close friend Rose, with a personality as vibrant as a beautiful rose and natural red hair as well, to help organize a hair transformation party at a wig shop—not a common event in 2004.

Within only a few days, Rose notified and assembled thirty fabulous, fun women friends to gather at the wig shop, snack on appetizers, drink wine, talk, laugh, and cry while Bonnie, the wig lady, cut off my hair and styled the very top section into a really cool Mohawk. I gritted my teeth before I looked in the mirror to see my bare head. I said, "Bonnie, please put my wig on. I look like a shaved sheep, and I feel naked without hair." One of my friends was doing a documentary on dealing with cancer, and had her film crew shoot scenes during the party.

When the roots of my hair fell out after my first chemo, everything had moved so fast, I didn't have time to think about the effects of treatment. My head was sore and tender. I wore caps or scarves at home and wigs when I went to work. A couple times, when driving to work, I looked in the car mirror and noticed my red cotton nightcap still on my head. I just had to laugh. I soon learned to always have an extra wig in the car.

The effects after each toxic chemo cocktail—Cytoxan, Adriamycin (aka the Red Devil), and Taxatere—were awful. It was like having a near-death experience similar to those I'd only read about. I felt I was out of my body and wished like hell I was. I lost twelve pounds, mostly from not wanting to eat or drink anything. My throat was raw; my mouth was full of sores. I found it hard to swallow Ensure, a nutrition drink that my nutritionist had recommended. My children helped keep my attitude up. Jessica flew to Austin to go to chemo with me and Katie, an oncology nurse, convinced me "to take care of my body first, and not even think that I was wasting my time sleeping and not working." She said, "Sleeping is your job now."

A mohawk moment during the head shaving party

The day after each chemo infusion, I had to go into the cancer center for a Neulasta shot to help create white blood cells and boost my immune system. The shot took about a minute and felt like a bolt of lightning shooting through me. I felt nauseous and dizzy. I fainted a couple of times. When I became conscious, I would be attached to an EKG machine, and was being administered oxygen with an IV because my blood pressure had fallen dramatically. I dreaded each chemo because the effects of the treatments were cumulative.

70

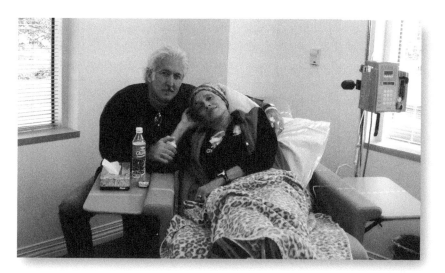

Brent and I cuddling during chemo

During my recovery process, I had bad dreams, where I was locked in a dark room with needles coming at me from all directions. I'd wake up suddenly and everything looked blurry. No longer being strong enough to jog made me despondent. I lay in bed, worried about the barrage of exorbitant medical bills that arrived regularly. I had no energy to deal with the medical insurance companies. I quit listening to depressing news of well-known people dying from cancer, including, Dana Reeve, Peter Jennings, Ed Bradley, Ann Richards, and Molly Ivins.

Brent took off work and waited on me hand and foot, taking care of my every need. He made sure I drank water consistently. He put lemon or lime flavors in it to camouflage the metallic taste. He served me soft foods on red plates to make me smile. He gave me plastic forks to lesson the tinny taste and salt water to help prevent mouth sores. He helped me to the shower when I was losing it from both ends at the same time. He listened, rather than trying to fix.

So many people reached out in a multitude of ways from sending hundreds of cards, letters, and emails with heartfelt wishes, to staying with me and walking my English springer spaniel. Others sent or delivered plants and bouquets of flowers, music CDs, humorous videos, books, and original poems. Some people I didn't even know brought me homemade soups, breads, and healing dishes. And friends designed homemade earrings, pendants, special pieces of art as well as their own priceless stones and special crystal healing items. I appreciated the scented candles, journals, head turbans, scarves, pajamas, body lotion, mineral baths, tea, Beanie Babies, talking dolls and angels in many shapes and material. I was overwhelmed with the outpouring of love and kind words that gave me strength. I vowed when I was better to thank each one for their thoughtfulness and generosity.

I used my humor to alleviate my fear of the unknown. I would point to my port-a-cath receptor protruding on the right side of my chest and say, "Push this spot and listen to the song." When they pressed it, I would sing a happy refrain from a song like, "Here Comes the Sun" by the Beatles.

It took about a year before I began to wake almost every day, feeling energized, realizing I had been given another day to live.

I didn't know this was only the beginning of what was to come. ❁

PenCharrette and Pen Pals

"This gal is a #1 Montblanc seller! Will you marry me?"

I'd received a lot of positive online feedback messages from thousands of pen buyers, but this one—my first marriage proposal—caught my eye. I chuckled.

Eric from Canada told me he wrote the comment because he said he could tell that I liked to laugh and also appreciated my prompt customer follow-up. I sell Montblanc pens now and many of my customers have become pen pals including: Matilda in South Africa, Reef in Australia, Tigran in Sweden, Earl in England, Gunnar in Iceland, Edison in Indonesia, and many more. My online friends around the world are a delightful and welcome benefit of my Montblanc pen business, called PenCharrette on eBay.

I wanted a way to apply the entrepreneurial skills that I had nurtured during my thirty-five year career in the business world. In 2007, my intense cancer treatments rendered me forgetful, exhausted, and unable to continue working my full-time executive job, but what could I do with little energy and memory loss? I felt myself spiraling downward, unproductive, and no longer connected globally. Then, like magic, Brent and my daughter Jessica suggested that I sell some of our household items and personal belongings online. Jessica taught me how to use eBay—a demanding teaching task indeed with my chemo brain. I kept forgetting what she explained.

It all started slowly, but eventually I sold sweaters, key chains, watches, pocketknives, computer monitors, purses, cell phones, jewelry, cameras, sunglasses, coats, suitcases—and one Montblanc mechanical pencil. Eighteen years earlier, Brent had purchased the pencil for his design projects, but he no longer used it. Meticulous, he had kept it in pristine condition.

My description said, "Ideal for those who like a handcrafted, precisely balanced, and durable pencil for writing, drawing, sketching or designing.

You can use this to be the next van Gogh, Agatha Christie, Hemingway, or Frank Lloyd Wright." This listing, unbeknownst to me at the time, foreshadowed my soon-to-be business, buying, refurbishing, marketing, and selling Montblanc writing instruments and accessories on eBay.

With that first pencil, I had buyers from three countries offer to pay a higher price within a few minutes of posting my listing. I wondered why. I did tons of research and discovered a global demand for these fine, German pens that had been produced for more than one hundred years. I'd learn that these writing instruments appeal to men and women alike, as they exemplify quality, timelessness, and sophistication. They also fit into free standard mailing boxes. Even when refurbished, they retain value. eBay gave me an outlet to use my business skills, satisfy my passion for writing, and be productive.

Communicating with customers multiple times is vital to my eBay success. I correspond with each buyer a minimum of five times. I answer questions before the sale, send a thank-you right after the purchase, insert a thank-you note in the package, provide the tracking number in a follow-up email, and finally give customer feedback on eBay. I like feeling I add value and help others fulfill their dreams. One customer commented, "Your fair pricing made it possible for me to own my first Montblanc pen, which I've wanted for years."

My buyers range from professors, bankers, accountants, and ranchers to morticians, ministers, attorneys, writers, doctors, and travel agents. Their purchase patterns reflect the economic situation in their countries. When a particular currency is stronger than the dollar, people in those countries are more apt to buy Montblanc high-end pens.

I'm very intrigued by the psychological reasons people buy and use different pens. Matilda in South Africa, who prefers the Writer's Edition Pens, especially the 'Agatha Christie Fountain,' said, "I slow down in a Zen-like way and have a sense of contentment writing with an instrument that has historical meaning, rather than writing on a computer." Reef in Australia, wrote, "I feel my body and mind unwind when I use my 'Special Edition John Lennon Ballpoint.' I especially like the intimacy of connecting with the paper. For me, it's like painting on the page."

I love to receive emails like these. They confirm I represent the exceptional brand that Montblanc is. I feel honored that my pen pals trust me, and they value my friendship and my knowledge about the various styles of these pens. We exchange holiday cards and communicate by email often. I

am most uplifted and grateful when I read my 100% positive customer feedback rating in all eBay categories. Here are a few of the thousands of positive
comments I've received from buyers in seventy-seven countries during the
past eight years.

"AMAZING, SWEET, HELPFUL seller who CARES about her customers."

"The Best Seller in the world. Greetings from Spain."

"eBay is a better place because of Deena. Always the Gold standard."

"Very reliable and honest seller. Seamless transaction. The BEST!!!

Some people ask, "Doesn't your business cause you stress?"

"No, it's flexible so I can work around my treatment schedule. It is great
therapy for me and gives me a way to stay engaged in the world and the
wonderful people in it." 🏵

Orders for Montblanc pens ready to pack up and mail

Crime Scene in the Kitchen

*B*lood spurted everywhere, on the cupboards, counters, walls, my clothes, the cooked salmon, and my top and white pants. It looked like a horrid murder scene.

I was confounded, not because our dinner party had turned macabre, but because I was shocked that when Brent walked in and saw what happened, he was not his usual calm self. He screamed, "I can't take this anymore. I'm losing Deena piece by piece!"

I joked, "But the best piece is still here!" He didn't laugh. But I know my guardian angels chuckled. I had recently lost part of my boob, my hair, my eyebrows, eyelashes, and my toenails from chemo.

Now, the top of the ring finger on my right hand to the first knuckle was missing. I hadn't felt a thing. I had no pain, although the sight was gruesome, not for the faint of heart. I held my hand straight up above my head to help stop the bleeding, while Brent grabbed a washcloth and wrapped it tightly around my hand and shouted, "Someone find Deena's finger!"

I had never ever seen Brent freak out. Since the onset of my cancer diagnosis, the surgeries, chemotherapy, and radiation sessions, he'd appeared levelheaded, and unflappable. Until now.

It was 2005 and we'd invited two young couples to our home for an evening dinner to celebrate the end of my initial cancer treatments. One couple brought their family dog, a golden retriever, whom I agreed was okay to bring. Our gentle and submissive English springer spaniel, Soho got along well with other furry pals.

We started talking and enjoying our appetizers on the back porch overlooking the lush hill country. After a while, I opened the closed sliding glass doors to the living room and went back to the kitchen to check on the dinner. Both dogs followed me. I took the salmon from the oven and put the tray on the counter. In an instant, I saw the golden, whom I've since nicknamed Chopper, biting Soho in the neck. I yanked Chopper off him.

Without warning, Chopper bit off the tip of my finger, right below the nail bed. It flew somewhere in the kitchen.

Chopper's owner found my finger and put it directly on ice. We learned later that a finger should be kept cold, never put on ice; however, in this case it wouldn't have mattered anyway. With the finger part in a baggie, Brent rushed me to Seton Hospital Emergency Center fifteen minutes away. The other couple saw blood dripping from Soho's neck and rushed him to the emergency veterinarian.

At Seton, there happened to be an orthopedic hand specialist on call. Brent and I interpreted that to mean that finger accidents must occur often. We thought my finger could be reattached.

The hand surgeon arrived in about half an hour and Brent handed him my finger tip. Examining my hand, he said tersely, as if in a hurry, "I need to cut off the top part of your finger,

My sweet Soho

otherwise you could get gangrene. Parts bitten off by any animal can not be reattached." With surgical instruments in hand, he inserted the first needle in my finger to numb it. I let out a piercing shriek that sounded like a screaming cat just caught by a coyote. The doctor said, "Quit acting like a baby." I wanted to give him the finger, but he was working on my hand. Apparently, interrupting his Friday night did not sit well with him.

Now composed, Brent said, "If you please, my wife has just finished months of chemo and radiation treatments."

The doctor asked, "Who is your medical oncologist? Who is your radiation oncologist?" Brent told him. Instantly, this information softened the doctor's manner. He said our medical oncologist lived in his neighborhood. He mustered a smidgen of compassion and then he inserted another needle into my finger while Brent held my other hand.

The pain was excruciating! My tears plopped to the floor. I made no sounds. When the finger was finally numbed, he cut it straight off below the nail and proficiently sewed the skin together. He sanitized and bandaged the area securely. He wrote a prescription for pain pills.

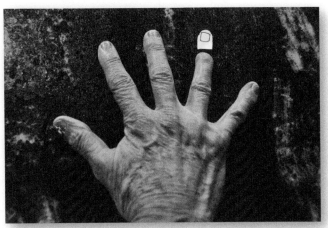

*My homemade paper prosthetic didn't do much,
but it made me feel better.*

I asked him, "Can I please have my finger? I would like to keep it." He gave it back to me. I preserved it in a plastic container with formaldehyde and stored it in a bathroom cupboard.

Regularly, in the morning before work, I went to finger therapy sessions for an hour. This went on for a couple of months. I learned various finger exercises to help regenerate new nerves, so my finger would feel again. Over the course of a year, I trained my other fingers to compensate. Whenever I hit a nerve on my bandaged finger, I would yelp like a dog. I

78

often experienced what is known as phantom finger phenomenon, where one feels the finger still there.

I never appreciated my ring finger until I lost part of it. I'd pick up a box, a plate or a cup and drop it. I couldn't play the piano for a long time and had to learn to compensate with other fingers. I could no longer squeeze anything, like toothpaste, out of a tube. When I did pushups, I learned to balance with just four fingers. When I went to the nail salon for a trim, I glibly asked for a discount because I only had nine nails.

For several years after the accident, if people asked me what happened, I said that my hand got caught in a heavy door and broke my finger. I never wanted to give dogs a bad reputation. Besides, who would believe a golden retriever was the culprit? I will go to almost any lengths to protect dogs from those who don't like them. By not divulging what really happened, I could avoid listening to people say things like, "That's why I don't like dogs. You can't trust them."

The owners never apologized, but they did pay Soho's vet bill. I speculated that since the wife was an attorney, she nor her husband wanted their words—even an apology—to ever be used against them. We never took any legal action.

In my quest to find out more about finger accidents, I learned that few finger losses are dog related. Most are caused by power tools and occur more often to men than women. About 30,000 people, both kids and adults, are rushed to US emergency rooms each year because of an amputated finger. Nearly seventy percent of finger amputations must be completely severed, just as mine was.

I used the loss of my finger as a source of humor. I joked that I was going to sell the piece on eBay. People would gasp, put their hands over their mouths and say crazy things like, "Oh Deena! Isn't that illegal?" Or "Someone could get your DNA and frame you as a murderer." In 1999, someone did try to sell a body part—a kidney—on eBay. The bidding went into the millions before the company realized what was happening and stopped the auction.

Every now and then, I take my finger out of the Tupperware container, stored in a bathroom cupboard, to look at it. The appearance has changed. There is a vine-like vein that has grown almost three inches.

My friend's ten-year-old daughter wanted to see it and when she looked at it, she commented, "Creepy Cool! This would make a funny decoration on our Halloween door wreath. Wait a minute, maybe not because an animal could jump up and eat it!"

Those who knew that my mother saved her uterus in a Kerr jar say, "You are a chip off the old block."

Brent said, "I never want to look at that thing again." ✾

Motherly Instinct

That looks like a teensy animal in the street. Is it a cat? A dog? Whatever it is, I'd better stop so I don't run over it, I thought to myself.

I slammed on the brakes. My German shorthaired pointer, who had been standing in the back of my SUV, tumbled forward, hit the back of the front seat and stood back up again. I quickly got out of my car, leaving the front door wide open. I raised my arms high, waved my hands back and forth and jumped up and down like a crazy person. I stopped the traffic coming from both sides of a major four-lane street.

Just two blocks away, kids and parents were walking across the street af-ter school had let out at three o'clock. I raced to the front of my car. Underneath the bumper I saw a tiny, white-spotted fawn, thin and only about a foot tall. He looked at me with his brown eyes, oversized in proportion to his small head. I guessed him at no more than three or four days old.

My motherly instinct clicked in. I glanced on both sides of the street and saw a deer standing on the opposite side. I pulled the fawn up on all four legs and tried to push him toward the deer. His body weak, he immediately went splat on the pavement.

Since he wasn't strong enough to hold himself up on his gangly legs, I tried to lift him, putting my arms

Safe at last

81

around his tummy to carry him quickly across the street so as not to hold up traffic long. He slithered out of my hands like a worm. Light as a small bag of flour, he probably weighed close to five pounds. I picked him up. Again, he slipped through my hands. Plop! He didn't make a sound. His body quivered.

My mind rushed. *The only way to get him to the sidewalk is to push him. I cupped my hands under his back end and gently held him up by his wobbly back legs.* I pushed him inch-by-inch, wheelbarrow style, to the sidewalk where his mother immediately licked him and with her nose, pushing him to the grassy area. Thankfully, she did not reject the fawn because of my human scent. I hurried back to my car.

This entire incident took only about a minute. It seemed longer. No one had honked. No car had moved. I saw eight or more cars in front of me lined up behind my car. Grateful that no one had gotten out and started yelling at me, in retrospect, I thought, *They must have figured that staying in their cars was safer.* The people in front could see I was pushing the fawn to safety. When drivers started passing by me from the opposite direction, some glanced over and smiled.

Though abruptly stopping traffic in the middle of one of Austin's busiest neighborhood streets was risky, I felt good saving a newly born animal. I believe that had I not stopped, the fawn could have been run over. With the heavy traffic and his small size, I doubt anyone would have seen him in time to save him. Reuniting him safely with a deer that must have been his mother, made that beautiful day in May even more wonderful. ❀

Chilled to the Bones

*O*n a sunny day in May 2006, during a brief friendly exchange with our oncologist, I held Brent's hand and my heart pounded loudly, beating steady like a metronome as we waited to hear the results of my last scan. I felt apprehensive. Anxious, but hopeful as always, I almost fainted when Dr. Tucker gave us the diagnosis.

I just had a guided needle bone biopsy and body imaging scans—a PET (Positron Emission Tomography) and CAT (Computed Axial Tomography)— because my cancer markers had shot up three times higher than my last scans only three months earlier. These revealed the cancer had spread to multiple bones, including my ribs, spine, and ilium. I had several fractures.

Bewildered and chilled to my bones, I sat motionless. No one spoke for what seemed like minutes. I thought, *I'm glad I don't have his job. I would not want to give people bad news like oncologists have to do.* In a trembling voice, I asked, "Is this serious?"

Our oncologist softly answered, "Yes." Numb with fear, I held back my tears. On my previous visit, I mentioned I had tripped and fallen several times for no apparent reason. Now it all made sense. Some of the bones had weakened from metastatic cancer.

Since there is no Stage V, my anxiety heightened knowing I had Stage IV, the final stage. Hadn't I finished seven intense rounds of chemo just fifteen months earlier in 2004? Why had all those rounds of toxic chemo — Taxotere, Cytoxan and Adriamycin (the Red Devil)- and weeks of radiation, and surgeries not killed the cancer? I thought I'd defeated the Grim Reaper. I didn't want to repeat that dreaded experience again.

After processing the diagnosis, we realized we must face our nemesis head-on once again. Brent and I asked tons of questions, "Why hadn't the cancer in my bones shown on scans before now?" "Will I need the Red Devil chemo again?" "Is there a cure?" "How long do I have left to live?"

Compassionate, our oncologist answered our questions gently, but directly and did not sugarcoat anything. He explained that cancer can only be detected in bones when a cell mass is large enough to show up on scans—a minimum of one million cancer cells. He said, "There is no cure for cancer yet, but I can develop an ongoing treatment program to help manage it." He could not say for sure how long or if the drugs would work, but his immediate action plan gave us hope.

Grateful for the many bouquets from friends and family

Brent and I decided that rather than start the dying process, I would take more chemo and believe it would work. This time around, my chemo cocktail consisted of Taxol, Carboplatin, Herceptin and Zometa. Each chemo treatment killed both good and bad cells and knocked me flat for at least a week. I got depressed. I couldn't recall ever being so weak.

Many of the days I lay in bed, sad and angry, because I felt my body had betrayed me. This contrast of peaks and valleys was difficult for me. I likened them to the time when Brent, Jessica, and I traveled from the highest peaks of Machu Picchu in Peru to the darkest depths of the Amazon Jungle in Bolivia. However, I, alone, had to experience this trek; no one could walk this for me. 🌸

It's All About the Wigs

*R*aspberry, teal, honey,
sky blue, or eggplant purple,
I keep a rainbow of wigs on a shelf
to light up the days
and retrieve my femininity.

When I lost my hair
and there was nothing there,
but scars and strays,
I bought vibrant wigs to match
the color of my favorite shoes
and cheer my gloomy days.

At the post office, the cafe, the market,
Like magic, people show up
out of nowhere
and comment or lend a hand.
 "Oh, I love your hair!"
"Who is your stylist?"
"What color would you say that is?"

I always reply
with a smile and a sparkle,
"Thank you for your kind words."

86

Wondering . . . Should I take off my wig
to show my whimsical side
and surprise them with my bald head?

That without chemo
radiation
and brain surgery,
I would never have known
the amazing joy and fun
I have with my silly
colorful wigs.

*A friend from my
cancer support group
requested we wear socks
to her funeral.
I coordinated mine
with a blue wig.*

African Odyssey

I looked high up at the dark brown, wide-set eyes keenly staring at me from a short distance. The tender lustrous gaze of the giraffe infused my whole being with intense love. His broad head and huge skyward-bound neck towered above the zebras and elephants lying under the humongous trunk of an African stunted, barren baobab tree. At approximately sixteen feet in height, the giraffe seemed taller than the Jolly Green Giant statue in Blue Earth, Minnesota. Every part of his body was extra long, from his eyelashes to his face, neck, legs, and tail. His calm eyes pleaded, "Hug me. Hug me." He rhythmically swung his graceful neck like a pendulum and implored, "Please come over to me."

Feeling compelled to bond with him, I blurted out loud, "Come closer and bend down so I can pet you."

My mind rapidly scanned for the quickest way to get up to him. With no ladders or ropes in these sparsely vegetated plains, reaching that high was impossible. My heart pounded loudly, like the African djembe drums. I climbed up on the back of our open-roofed Rover jeep and wiped the dust off my face to see him better. My excitement took over. "I want to go pet him!" I exclaimed.

Too tall to touch

My husband said, "This is not a petting zoo. Any one of these animals could eat you alive." I sat down in my seat, knowing this gigantic brownish-black spotted giraffe had connected with me. I was ecstatic. It was like watching a National Geographic documentary, only this was real.

Four days earlier, Brent and I had landed at the Kilimanjaro International Airport in Tanzania with our longtime friends, Rita and Wayne. We felt awake and energized, thanks to the ticket agent in Austin, who, after reading my oncologist's note, gave us an extra seat for me to lie down during the twenty-some hour flight.

We were also grateful to Rita for teaching us the Qi Horary acupressure anti-jet lag technique. Every two hours during the flight, we'd pressed different points on our arms or legs with the end of a ballpoint, moving it back and forth twenty to thirty times, in short bursts of five strokes. This helped adjust our bodies' biological clocks to the African time zone.

Once on the ground, things had changed. "Brent, help me," I'd said. "I feel claustrophobic. I'm dizzy. My head is spinning." The stifling heat, crowds, chaos, and commotion in the terminal closed in on me. I held on tight to my wig. He led me to a quiet corner to sit down. He asked if I would be okay while he filled out our customs forms. I nodded yes and leaned against the wall. Taking deep breaths I calmed myself down just like I had done many times before I went into the claustrophobic scan tube for my brain radiation.

Very concerned about my taking such a taxing trip, my oncologist had raised his eyebrows when I said we were going on safari, as if to say, "Did I hear you correctly?" He did say, "Travel abroad means you will miss two treatments, but without treatment, you will not have any chemo side effects. It's your decision."

I said, "But this cancer could kill me. I'd better go to Africa while I'm alive." From the time I was little, I've wanted to see wild animals run free in a place like the Serengeti, uncontrolled by humans. Knowing me, my oncologist realized he couldn't change my mind and wrote a note that I could give to the airline agent requesting "extra consideration due to the extent and nature of the cancer."

While I rested against the airport wall, Brent, Rita and Wayne completed the customs forms. Brent held on to me as we went through customs and left the bustling airport. Wayne and Rita's twenty-nine-year-old son, John, and his girlfriend, Chelsea, were outside waiting for us. We hugged them and I took in deep breaths of the dry African air.

The drive from the airport to the town of Moshi—at the base of the Kilimanjaro Mountains and nicknamed the Roof of Africa—took about an hour. It was the dry season in the fall of 2009. We had driven through a sandstorm on the way.

Chelsea and John told us fascinating stories about their work in Tanzania. "I'm a volunteer librarian at the Moshi Amani School for street children," said Chelsea. John was doing field research for his doctorate on how AIDS impacts conservation efforts. In the few months John had lived in Africa, he had taught himself the local language, so he became our designated interpreter. He spoke Swahili so fluently that even the natives asked him, "Where do you live in our country?"

The first night, we stayed in a cozy Moshi hotel. Listening to marimba music and smelling the sweet Arabica coffee brewing, we talked in the hotel courtyard, under a canopy of scarlet flame trees and tall mvule trees. That night I told some silly jokes that made everyone laugh, so I decided to tell a couple every evening before dinner. Everyone loved this one.

> The 98-year-old Mother Superior from Poland was dying.
> The nuns gathered around her bed trying to make her last
> journey comfortable. They gave her some warm milk to
> drink but she refused. Then one of the nuns took the glass
> back to the kitchen. Remembering a bottle of Irish whiskey
> received as a gift the previous Christmas, she opened and
> poured a generous amount into the warm milk. Back at
> Mother Superior's bed, she held the glass to her lips. Mother
> Superior drank a little, then a little more and before they
> knew it, she had the whole glass down to the last drop.
> "Mother," the nuns asked earnestly, "Please give us some
> wisdom before you die." She raised herself up in bed and
> with a pious look on her face said, "Don't sell that cow."

In Moshi town, locals came up to us and asked, "Kutoka Obama land? Sisi ni furaha wewe alikuja hapa." ("You from Obama land? We are happy you came here.") Obama's larger-than-life image was displayed on buildings, cars and T-shirts. The Tanzanians revered him like a god and warmly welcomed us.

Before our safari, we flew from Moshi to Zanzibar, which is on the island of Uguia. We stayed in a charming hotel, only yards away from the white coral beach on the Indian Ocean. Children from the local village of Motemwe played on the white powdery sand beaches. They ran after us asking to see whatever we carried, shouting, "Let me see. Let me see."

A local woman gathering algae at low tide at the beach in Montemwe.

Brent shot incredible pictures of the local women gathering algae from the ocean and bundling it tightly to sell in the local marketplaces. With camera in tow, we drove a short distance to Stone Town in Zanzibar City, where he reveled in the eclectic architecture reflecting Swahili, Moorish, Arab, Persian, Indian, and European cultural influences.

The laid-back ambiance in Zanzibar did not prepare us for the reality of traversing the Serengeti. Instead of lazily waking up to coffee and breakfast served to us, we had to get up before dawn every morning. We rode in old Land Rovers, bouncing up and down across rutty gravel roads and rocky streams in order to see the animals in the early morning, the best time to see them. At times I was afraid my bones would break, as parts of some had been eaten away by the cancer. Each day, to shield ourselves from the relentless sun, we wore hats, sunglasses, long pants, and long sleeves.

Despite the brutal bone-jarring travel and intense heat, the amazing sights enthralled us. I had never experienced such an incredible place, the vastness of the open spaces, the impressionistic colors and shadows of the earth. I'd wave my hands above my head and shout, "I'm actually in Africa. This is not a dream." The reality of my adventure come true began to release me from the fear of dying. In spite of the harsh heat, I felt invigorated.

In the Serengeti, miles of national parks and intermittent lodging dot the seemingly infinite landscape. At the Tarangire Tented Safari Lodge, we slept in spacious tents built on wooden platforms with thatched roofs, en suite and nicely furnished. The views from the bluff overlooking the Tarangire River, wildlife and endless terrain were spectacular. I loved listening to the snuffing and roaring of the lions and the trumpeting of the elephants in the night.

Energized in the Serengeti

Walking back to our lodge one morning after breakfast, Brent and I felt something falling on our heads. Looking up, we saw monkeys in the tree eating chips. I said, "Bet they got into Wayne and Rita's room and stole our potato chips. Who'd have known monkeys like chips? Hurry Brent and get a picture." Brent grabbed his high speed Nikon camera, with the adjustable lens, hanging from his shoulder strap on his shoulder and took several shots of the monkeys.

The sight tickled my funny bone and I couldn't help but laugh. Cute black-faced monkeys with grizzled hair, looking like they're having the time of their life were chowing down the chips.

Vervet monkeys survey for chips and gin.

I wondered, *What else had they taken from the room*? Brent said, "Let's run to the tent to see if there are monkeys still in there." When we arrived, Wayne and Rita were already there. It looked like burglars had ransacked the place. Crackers, cookies, empty bags, and clear liquid covered the floor.

By the sound of Wayne's voice, one could tell he did not find the scene a bit funny.

"Damn it. Damn it. Damn it," he shouted. "They broke my only bottle of gin. The bottle is totally empty. I can't salvage any. What's left is on the floor. They drank most it. And there's nowhere to buy a bottle in the Serengeti. I shooed the last two monkeys, who were sitting on the bed eating like they owned the placed, out of here."

Apparently, while we were all at breakfast in the dining area of Tarangire Lodge, the monkeys had climbed in through the ventilation slots near the ceiling in the bathroom area and found the wicker box full of bags of food and drinks that Wayne had put up high on top of the dresser the night before.

We teased Wayne throughout the trip, exaggerating the monkey scene a bit every day. By the time we arrived home, the story had morphed into a wild tale where Wayne and Rita found three of the monkeys sleeping in their bed from hangovers, like the three bears in the Goldilocks story.

A couple of nights, we camped in the High Steppe Oldonyo Sambu wilderness area. Inside our super-cozy camp tents, we found thin single mattresses on the beds, a lantern and washbasin with water. Outside, about 150 feet away, we located the toilets and solar shower enclosures.

During the afternoons, we hiked on the mountain trails guided by Maasai men clad in colorful red and blue plaid sarongs. The women cooked our meals in black caldrons over fire pits, and upon our return the smells of baked beans, wali (rice), uagai (polenta), and chicken permeated the air.

After dinner, seated around a campfire with the screaming sounds of hyenas in the background, we listened to our Maasai guides—one had a Master's Degree in Agriculture from the United States—share their history, culture, and customs with us. They explained that the word Serengeti is derived from the Maasai language, "Maa" and "Serengit" meaning "endless plains." Easy to understand why because the plains, animals, and beauty stretched for miles in every direction.

When asked about their culture, Raziki, one of the guides, explained that the husband's family selects his future wife based on her work ethic, not on her beauty. "When the man owns at least eight cattle, he gives them to his bride-to-be as her dowry." Status is based on the number of cattle one owns. They told us that they use the cows' milk and blood for food. They use their hide for mattresses, shoes, and other items. They use their dung for plastering hut walls, and sterile urine for medicinal purposes. They do not eat them, except for special occasions.

The men may have several wives, whereas women marry once in a lifetime. If one of the wives dies, the remaining wives in the community raise the kids, so children will always have the protection of a loving home and family.

I didn't know the extreme danger that lurked in this remote area at night. I peeked out of our small plastic tent window and saw the moonlight shining on armed guards on the mountaintops holding high-powered .30-06 rifles, protecting us from lions, cheetahs, gazelles, and hyenas. Convinced we were safe, I zipped the window shut and slept peacefully.

Traveling deep into the Ngorongoro Crater, the largest unbroken caldera in the world, a UNESCO World Heritage Site, boggled my mind. From the top, looking down, I couldn't distinguish any life below. I never could have imagined that once we drove down the twelve-mile road, that spiraled the rim to the 165-square mile surface, I would see thousands of animals roaming freely along lakes, in rain forests, and on vast plains, plus archeological sites and Maasai villages. I felt like Alice in Wonderland as I entered an enchanting fantasy world.

Maasai are devoted to family and community.

We visited a remote Maasai village to see for ourselves many of the things our guides had told us. Women, children, and babies, huddled together in front of their huts, turned around and welcomed us with huge smiles. Three women, all wives of the same man, wore on their elongated earlobes long, dangly earrings made of string, colorful beads, and seeds. Their sandals, scooped like garden shovels, consisted of pieces of tires and woven leather laces. Barefoot children shyly approached us holding onto their mothers' skirts.

We introduced ourselves, shook the mothers' hands, and gave them small bags of Band-Aids, antiseptics, cotton tips, rolled gauze, salves, and sanitized hand wipes. Just in case we had an opportunity to visit a village, we had prepared enough supplies for at least twenty people, per John and Chelsea, who said these are the items they needed. Grateful for these gifts, the Maasai women smiled big and hugged us. Next, we gave baseball caps to the kids, who jumped up and down with excitement, danced around us tugging on our clothes, while the mothers waved their hands up to the sky in appreciation.

To show her gratitude, a woman welcomed us into one of the small huts, which had an open entry. We scrunched down and walked through the narrow, low portal into a small family area. She motioned all eight of us to sit on the wooden benches next to the walls. The ceilings were about five feet high. The room had no windows and was almost dark with just a stream of light coming through the open entry. There was an unlit fire pit and a wooden table, the only piece of furniture on the dirt floor.

The hut had two rooms in which the family did everything and kept their possessions. It reminded me of the secret dirt-floor underground hideaway, about 600 feet from our home in Cazenovia, that my brothers had dug for us kids to play in.

Raziki said, "The women build the huts. They use timber poles for the framework and weave a lattice of branches between the frames. They plaster them with a mix of mud, sticks, grass, ash and cow dung to keep the roof from leaking during the rainy seasons." He continued, "The circular fence around the Maasai village is made from the thorn branches of the acacia to keep the cows, sheep, and goats safe from the wild animals." I loved seeing and learning how the Maasai lived.

I chronicled every single species of animal, bird, tree, and plant we saw, 112 species in total. We watched leopards race to capture and kill wildebeests, dragging them up into the trees to eat. We spied on hippos, lions, cheetahs, buffalo, zebras, kudus, warthogs, gazelles, giraffes, monkeys and a plethora of exotic birds. We waited and waited with bated breath as the jackals and hyenas chased each other back and forth. Fast as lighting, they fought over a flamingo the hyenas had seized in midair. The jackals grabbed the remains and the hyenas ran in the opposite direction.

We observed families of elephants, who lovingly protected their babies in the center of their parades. I have always loved elephants because of their intelligence and loyalty to their families. I have a large collection of elephant figurines from around the world—many were gifts—displayed in our glass vintage lawyer bookcases. Surprisingly, on safari, I found myself drawn to the giraffes more than the elephants.

Brent took incredible photos of every species we saw.

I didn't want this magical Tanzanian adventure to end. Brent took thousands of poetic photos to recapture our time there. On the flight home, I watched *Out of Africa*. Before we started the trip, Brent and I worried about my health. We hoped I would survive the demanding expedition. To alleviate our concern, we had an emergency service, just in case I needed to be airlifted out.

I came home feeling better than usual, determined to live with purpose. My memories of the trip continue to sustain me through my endless treatment regimen and remind me to embrace adventure always. ❀

Twenty-Two Times
in the Torture Chamber

*E*ach time, the heavy helmet pressed tightly over my face, and the eight clamps securing it to the radiation table seemed to yell, "Clank. Clank. Clank. Clank," like metal prison doors slamming shut.

The plaster helmet, which looked like Hannibal Lector's mask, was formed especially for me. With a bit in my mouth, I couldn't move my lips, cheeks, or any part of my face. My feet bound with wide bands, I lay still on the radiation table, waiting for the stereotactic radiology treatment, wondering why the cancer had spread to my brain just two years after spreading to my bones.

I heard voices say, "You're doing great. You can do this."

"Don't move, not even an iota. There is no room for error."

You'll be finished in no time."

I wasn't allowed to take any drugs, because I had to be awake to hear the technicians.

Claustrophobic and terrified, I felt trapped. I thought, *Maybe this is how people feel when they are buried alive. What if one of the radiation techs dies and my brain gets burned up?*

When the radiation started, the electromagnetic eyes rotated around my head while the laser beams zapped the cancer tumors in my brain. I froze with anxiety. I said to myself, I must change my thoughts before I go crazy.

I imagined that Oprah had given me a room full of money and I had just a few minutes to decide what I would do with it, otherwise I would lose the money. This worked. I gave the money away to dog shelters, children who had cancer, and single women with children rebuilding their lives. By the time the radiation ended, I hadn't spent it all. I decided to use this same visualization next time and give money to my husband to take me on trips to Rome, Barcelona, or Sidney to see great architecture.

I smiled inside when I heard, "You're done Mrs. Byers."

I continued to have "scanxiety" before each radiation session and dreaded each time lying on the table, convincing myself to think of anything that would take my mind off being in the torture chamber. One year, I had ten consecutive brain-radiation sessions, each fifteen minutes. Another year, I had twelve, each ten minutes.

The effects from radiating my breast and bones had been mild, with only a little burning, compared to the effects of the brain radiation. Besides the traumatic sessions, my brain radiation caused permanent hearing loss, and now I wear hearing aids. I really don't mind them because of the benefits. I use texting and messaging, since I can't hear all the words when talking on the phone. If I turn my aids

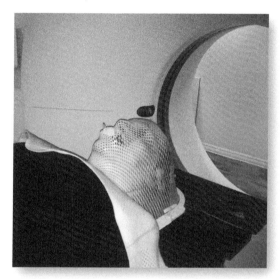

Not my idea of fun

off, I can silence annoying conversations, and best of all, when I take them out, I can go right to sleep because I can't hear a sound.

A few months after my last brain radiation, a PET scan of my body showed cancer had reappeared in my bones again and shortly after, my brain MRI revealed one of my lesions had tripled in size. My radiation oncologist, Dr. Tim Dziuk, could not determine if the lesion was more cancer or radiated cells that had grown. He conferred with my medical oncologist, Dr. Hellerstedt, and they determined I should immediately go to a brain surgeon.

Brent and I learned from the surgeon that radiated dead cancer cells could be as terminal as cancer cells because anything that's growing in the brain can impact key body functions. If the mass was cancer and I did nothing, my shelf life was three to five months. If the mass was growing scar tissue, it could keep on growing and death would be inevitable, but could be very debilitating. Without brain surgery, most likely some of my key organs could stop working.

I wanted to live, so we opted for surgery. ✿

Embraced by one of my heroes before her show

No Loose Screws

I saw human-like forms, maybe four or five, all dressed in white, floating around me. Their kind, warm eyes, of various shapes and colors, enveloped me. They asked questions very slowly.

"Do you know where you are?"

"No. Am I in heaven?"

"You are in the hospital. You are out of surgery."

"What is your name?"

"Deena."

"Deena, please wiggle your toes."

"Okay."

"Deena, now please wiggle your fingers."

I didn't hear or see anything else. I fell back asleep. When I woke up in the Intensive Care Unit, Brent said, "Deena, your brain surgery is over. The neurosurgeon, nurse, nursing assistant, and anesthesiologist have come to talk to you. The operation went well and you are doing great."

"Am I alive? Or dreaming?"

"Yes. You are alive."

To prepare for the operation, the nursing staff shaved and sanitized the right side of my head. After my anesthesia took hold, my brain surgeon, Dr. Craig Kemper, made a skin incision, pulled up my scalp and clipped it. He used a special medical drill to burr holes in my skull and removed a piece of bone flap, which he set aside. An MRI guided him to the exact place in my brain. After removing the mass, he fastened the bone section back in place with eight titanium screws—now permanent fittings in my skull—and stapled my scalp closed with eighteen heavy-duty surgical staples. The operation lasted four hours, including six pathology tests, conducted during the surgery.

"He did a precise job putting the staples on so evenly," Brent commented. I thought, *Would anyone else, other than an architect notice the exact alignment of the staples?*

Before the surgery, to ease the gravity of the situation, Brent had said, "Dr. Kemper, can you check for any loose screws too while you are in there?"

frankenstein's got
nothing on me.

I had asked the doctor to take pictures of the inside of my brain because I wanted to see what a mass looked like. To my surprise, the pictures revealed an off-white lumpy type of vegetable. Dr. Kemper confirmed the texture was similar to a piece of cauliflower.

I asked him if I had "a hole in my head" in place of the mass and, if so, would it ever fill in with other brain matter. "The hole will not fill in; it is permanent." He looked at Brent and said in his deadpan manner, "There are no loose screws."

Reading the surgeon's operative report, I found comfort in this line. "All sponge and needle counts were correct after procedure."

In the hospital, morphine and I became fast friends. I liked the euphoric feeling I had when taking it. Three days after surgery, I had to wean off morphine and take oxycodone for ten more days to manage my pain.

We were grateful to learn that the growing mass was scar tissue from the brain radiation, rather than more cancer. I learned this necrosis phenomenon occurs in only 5% of people who have radiated the cancer.

Each Christmas since the surgery, Brent and I sing a silly ditty to the tune, "All I Want for Christmas." Our version is, "All I want for Christmas is a craniotomy, a craniotomy, a craniotomy, all I want for Christmas is a craniotomy, so we can wish you a very merry Christmas!"

This surgery did not cure my cancer, as there is no cure yet, only chemo treatments to slow and manage progression. My treatments are never ending. I label myself a "chemo schlepper," having spent so many days in the chemo room over the years with my bag in tow, stuffed with my warm blanket, headsets, newspaper, writing journal, pens, books, snacks, and lip-gloss.

I've lived beyond the average five-year survival time for Stage IV breast cancer patients. I don't know why. Maybe luck. Maybe faith. Maybe drugs. Maybe my great oncologists. Maybe the love of my family, friends, and dog. Maybe no stress anymore. Maybe laughter. Maybe exercise. Maybe my support group. Maybe red wine.

What I do know is that I intend to be one of the few who live beyond a decade with Stage IV.

Wine, Women and Words

"This sure is a murky stew of a religion," Nancy said. "Seems like Hubbard took concepts from the Buddhist and Hindu religions, changed the names, and then mixed it with science fiction theories."

"I found the revelations in this book shocking and disturbing. This seems more like a cult than a religion." I added.

"Aren't all religions some form of cult?" Stacy commented.

"Depends on the definition. To say all religions are like this one is an overstatement. It's not like the ones I know," Adrienne said.

"For me the book is brilliant, though bizarre," said Rose. "Wright's research illustrates that people desperately want to believe in something, anything. I took away that even though Scientology is what it is now, who's to say that in a hundred years or so, it might be a totally new cosmic type of religion?"

This is some of the stimulating discussion we had about the book *Going Clear: Scientology, Hollywood, and the Prison of Belief,* by Lawrence Wright. In book club, everyone shares her perceptions or insights. In fact, we thrive on the varying viewpoints because when someone sees the same event and situation in a different light, the discussions always get provocative, even fiery at times. Sometimes we get so involved and vociferous that our moderator, Nancy, must get us back on track and say, "Let's not all talk at once; it's her turn now," pointing at one of us in the group.

Mastermind and organizer, Nancy started the book club in 2007. She must have had people like me in mind when she came up with the name, "Wine, Women and Words." Without hesitation, I accepted the invitation to join from one of her friends because the name captured what I love and enjoy—meeting smart, fun women who love books and forging lasting friendships. Braggarts, dark rain clouds and know-it-alls aren't tolerated, but that doesn't mean we don't speak up and say what we think. We do, but in a respectful manner.

Since the first meeting of nine of us, there are now twenty-six women—teachers, entrepreneurs, attorneys, artists, authors, writers and corporate, social and civic leaders—who are committed to keeping the book club viable and strong. We're democratic; we all vote to pick the six books we'll read a year in advance.

Book Club Christmas 2013

This past year, dubbed "Year of the Authors," we invited authors of the books we'd read to speak to us about their reasons for writing their books and the processes they went through. Among the memorable authors was Jesse Sublett, a tall, thin Texan musician with an easy manner, who spoke with candor and grace about his poignant memoir *Never the Same Again: a Rock 'n' Roll Gothic.*

First, Jesse sang two heartfelt bluesy rock-like songs in his gritty tone. When he talked about how he mustered up the courage to write about the murder of his girlfriend in 1976 by a serial murderer, he said, "I don't believe in the artificial concept of 'closure,' but as a writer, you write in order to figure things out, to discover what really happened, to resolve the puzzles and problems that tend to obscure the real story."

He continued, "In the process of investigating the often debilitating facts surrounding those events from over twenty-five years ago, and then turning them into a coherent, readable narrative, I found a measure of peace from some of the noise and nightmares that had haunted me all those years. I was able to forgive my younger self for some of the thoughtless things I had done;

I was even able to feel some sympathy for the disturbed mind who had visited these horrors on me and all the loved ones of his victims."

We enjoyed his wit and humor when he shared with us, "One thing about having Stage IV throat cancer is that when I started singing again, I ended up with the kind of bluesy, gravelly voice I had always wanted. Like they say, 'What the hell, I've got a right to sing the blues.'"

On the second Wednesday of every other month, a member hosts the meeting in her home; each time anywhere from twelve to twenty women attend. We start the evening with a lively social gathering, sometimes poolside, catching up on each other's lives, laughing, drinking wine, and eating the food we've each brought—dishes to complement the theme of the book and the country or era in which it's set. The group has a reputation for being intellectually stimulating and incredibly fun, and all remember to bring a bottle of wine. We even receive resumes from people who want to join, but we had to cap membership a year ago to keep the group from getting too big.

Over the past eight and a half years, our club has read at least fifty-five books of most genres, from *The Paris Wife* and *An Object of Beauty* to *The Goldfinch, Eclipse, Remarkable Creatures,* and *Abraham Lincoln: Vampire Hunter.* Some of the books I would never have selected to read had they not been chosen, but I'm so glad I did. I learned about cultures, ideas, relationships, and beliefs I had not known and now want to experience.

I lean toward nonfiction books, because I savor how authors express an emotion, in a succinct, visual way, like in *Eat, Pray, Love* when Elizabeth Gilbert wrote, "I want God to play in my bloodstream the way sunlight amuses itself on the water. ❀

Angels Among Us

*E*ven during the scariest times of my childhood and the most painful experiences I've had as an adult, I've felt angels with me. They have been and are my constant companions, whom I talk to daily.

The Oxford English Dictionary defines a guardian angel as "an angel conceived as watching over or protecting a particular person or place," and cites one of the term's earliest English uses in 1631, from the poet John Donne's, "The Relique," a poem about spiritual and physical love.

My angels protect and provide for me in many ways. They comfort me. They talk to me. They help me find my car keys. I'm sure I've exasperated them over the years, but they have never abandoned me. I believe that they have blessed my marriage to Brent. We have small and large angel figurines and mementos around our home, reminding us of their omnipresence.

Our first angel holiday card

Every year, Brent and I design a Holiday card depicting an angel that we feel is inspiring and encouraging, and that communicates our loving hopes for family and friends. Some of our favorites include: "The Angel of Music and Harmony" and "The Angel of New Beginnings." I come up with the concept and text, and Brent designs every card, creating the image I'm visualizing. We send out hundreds of cards to the many people who are angels in our lives.

angel of gratitude and celebration

Let's be thankful and celebrate

Some of the holiday angel cards we created to send our friends and family.

angel of music and harmony

angel of new beginnings

Allow your soul to sing songs of joy

You
Can Make All Possible in 2006

My Drug Dictionary

$\mathcal{P}$re cancer, had anyone said that someday I would be taking a truck-load of drugs to stay alive, I would have said, "Not me. I'd die before I'd ever become a druggie."

Since my initial diagnosis and throughout my treatment regimen for Triple Positive Breast Cancer that metastasized to my bones and brain, I've taken enough drugs—some daily, some weekly, others less often—to make one's head spin.

Peruse this list of some of the drugs that have helped keep me alive for eleven years—nine of those with Stage IV. I find it liberating to share my side effects not mentioned on patient information sheets, websites, or pharmacy labels.

Those who have taken or are now taking some of these drugs—and those who are druggies—may also be having amusing or tough experiences, like I am.

Adriamycin (A•dri•a•my•cin) *Aka* the Red Devil. This toxic chemo drug was a living hell! Felt like I was the girl in *The Exorcist*, vomiting, head spinning, and priest slapping included.

Ambien (Am•bi•en) No need to count sheep.

Ativan (At•i•van) Reduces anxiety and inhibitions. Liberates wardrobe and accessory choices.

Arimidex (A•rim•i•dex) An aromatase inhibitor to prevent production of estrogen. Side effects include back pain, hot flashes, screaming, and every other thing I hated about menopause.

Carboplatin (Car•bo•pla•tin) Potent chemo infusion. Killed some tumors and other U.G.Os (unidentified growing objects).

Cymbalta (Cym•bal•ta) Treats depression, chronic pain, and neuropathy. A large capsule in two unattractive colors.

Cytoxan (Cy•tox•an) Taken in combination with Taxotere and Adriamycin. Kills all cells, both good and bad, with added benefit of vomiting, pooping, and taking a shower simultaneously.

Decadron (Dec•a•dron) Reduces inflammation in the brain and halts hallucinations of talking teddy bears.

Darvocet (Dar•vo•set) Relieves moderate pain; but sadly, I don't do anything in moderation.

Estrace (Es•trace) Rymes with 'not in my face.' When cancer drugs dry one out and K-Y Jelly just doesn't cut it, it's time for a prescription of an industrial strength lube. Available in tubes, buckets, or my favorite— a 50 gallon drum.

Faslodex (Fas•lo•dex) Slows or stops the spread of hormonal breast cancer. Unoriginal side effects.

Heparin (Hep•ar•in) Prevents blood clots in the brain. Can cause necrotic skin lesions, which are useful for adding authenticity to zombie Halloween costumes.

Herceptin (Her•cep•tin) Treats aggressive HER2-Positive metastatic breast cancer. Revolutionary lifesaver. Served as a cocktail infusion with other chemo drugs and choice of olive or maraschino cherries.

Hydrocodone (Hy•dro•co•done) A codeine painkiller. Sometimes available in prescription cough syrup or for sale at bus stops.

Hydrocortisone (Hy•dro•cor•ti•sone) Rectal suppository for hemorrhoids and unspecified anal itching. If you want a party in your ass, this is the drug for you.

Kadcyla (Kad•cy•la) My recent chemo cocktail is a molecular targeted therapy drug, known as the smart bomb. Kadcyla searches and finds the cancer cells, then blows them up. My personal drone with a cruise missile. Have mild side effects: nose bleeds, dry mouth and fatigue.

Keflex (Kef•lex) Prevented infections after my brain surgery. The younger, edgier form of penicillin.

Keppra (Kep•pra) Foils post-craniotomy seizures. Made me dumb as a post.

Lexapro (Lex•a•pro) My daily dose of happiness, which helps maintain marital peace.

Levetiracetum (Lev•e•tir•ace•tum) Prevents seizures. A generic Keppra, which is harder to pronounce, but easier to get insurance approval for.

Lidocaine (Li•do•caine) Topical anesthetic for my port-a-cath. Keeps me from flying out of the chemo chair and punching the nurse when he or she sticks me with needles.

Lomotil (Lom•o•til) Stops incessant diarrhea. Note to self: Take before doing errands.

Lunesta (Lun•es•ta) Nighty-night everyone!

Marijuana (Mar•i•juan•a) Tried to ease pain. Didn't work. Made me sick. Keeps many cancer patients enjoying cartoons and sugary cereals.

Morphine (Mor•phine) My preferred pain-relieving drug. In my book, it's the rock star, top of the charts, all-time number one hit.

Neulasta (Neu•las•ta) One of the most painful autoimmune injections I've ever had. Thoroughly sucks. A couple of times I fainted like a Victorian lady with the vapors.

Nexium (Nex•i•um) Lessens gastroesophageal reflux. Protects stomach lining from chemo burn—or wanting to eat breakfast, lunch and dinner.

Oxycodone (Ox•y•co•done) For acute pain. Invites abuse by teen celebrities and self-prescribing physicians.

Percocet (Perc•o•cet) A great narcotic for severe pain. A must for aspiring junkies.

Phenergan (Phen•er•gan) For nausea, dizziness and motion sickness. Prescribed for chemo patients and people on discount cruises.

Prednisone (Pred•ni•sone) A steroid to prevent swelling in the brain, but not the thighs. A great way to get circus-lady big.

Taxotere (Tax•o•tere) Toxic chemo drug. Caused my toenails to fall off. Silver lining: no more need for pedicures.

Taxol (Tax•ol) Another toxic chemo drug. Caused classic cancer hair loss. Trade in expensive shampoo for cheap wigs and celebrate a permanent *Brazilian*.

Tykerb (Ty•kerb) Oral chemo that managed the cancer in my brain for a while, but gave me huge red sores all over my legs. Looked like I was wearing clown tights. Eating grapefruit increased the bad effects. Gave up all citrus for red wine.

Valium (Val•i•um) Strong antianxiety drug. Removed my paranoia about cancer and replaced it with a new paranoia about being killed by giant cockroaches instead.

Versed (Ver•sed) Induced short-term memory loss for my surgery. Did I say I had surgery?

Xanax (Xan•ax) I pop one of these anti-anxiety pills into my mouth before I go into my brain scans to keep me from screaming and flying out of the tube.

Xeloda (Xel•o•da) A dreaded chemo that made me super nauseous. Made me become a barf bag hoarder.

Zometa (Zo•me•ta) Stops new fractures caused by bone metastases. Keeps me pole vaulting and jumping over semis.

Zofran (Zo•fran) Prevents nausea. No side effects, no problems with drug interaction, and plays quietly in its room for hours.

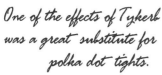

One of the effects of Tykerb was a great substitute for polka dot tights.

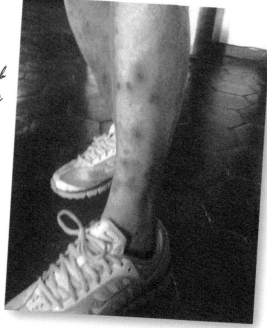

He Rescued Me

Unconditional and Loyal Love

*I*t was early morning in late August and I wasn't feeling well. I tried to lie down for a nap, but my German shorthaired pointer (GSP) kept pushing his nose into my face, sniffing at my mouth, constantly whimpering, pawing on my legs, as if trying to communicate something. This was not his normal behavior.

Usually, after eating, Dante would go outside and run like a streak of lightning in the yard around our house until he tired himself out. But he stuck to me like Velcro, not leaving my side. I didn't put it all together until a few days later when I read the results of my PET scan, confirming my cancer had returned in my bones. Apparently, he was trying to alert me that something was wrong.

Dante came into my life shortly after our gentle, sweet, loving ten-year-old English springer spaniel, Soho, died unexpectedly of kidney failure. I was so despondent; I thought he might have died first in order to be on the other side to welcome me. He took a piece of my heart with him. I wondered if his death was an omen that my time was near.

To buoy my spirits, Brent encouraged me to get online with him to search for a new companion. After we looked at several breeds, we decided the GSP fit our lifestyle and matched our key criteria: intelligent, affectionate, athletic, and easy to train. We found many people love this breed; in fact, there's a GSP group on FaceBook with 12,000 members, including me now. We also discovered the Texas GSP website that listed a gorgeous dog available for adoption in Austin. Brent called the agency volunteer, who came to our home to interview us and fill out an application to foster Dante. Within a few days, on my birthday, December 29, 2007, the volunteer brought Dante to our house.

Reticent and scared, he didn't look at us, rather looked down and stood hunched over, body shaking with his docked tail between his legs, like a scrawny character out of *Les Miserable*. He didn't respond to Harrison, the name given to him at the shelter, where he had spent three weeks. Once he became comfortable around us, we named him Dante after the Italian poet because he reminded us of a work of art, with his floppy, velvet ears, streamlined profile, dark chocolate face, and three very large evenly spaced chocolate spots on the back of his all-white body.

Apparently, a driver had spotted him running loose alongside a highway outside Houston, stopped, picked him up, and called animal rescue. A local vet estimated him to be two years old. Since Dante didn't like loud noises, we surmised he might have run away from the other hunting dogs and became disoriented.

We hired a dog trainer right away, which, turned out to be a wise decision. The trainer said, "The first thing we must teach him is his name, so he comes when you call him and learns that the commands are meant for him."

For the first week, I'd work for short periods with Dante, reinforcing his good behavior with treats and *that-a-boy* praises, until I had no doubt he would come when called. Once he learned his name, Dante quickly picked up the basic commands, "sit, stay, down, here, heel, halt, drop it." He had a laser memory. Once taught a command, it stuck. In no time he captured our hearts and we adopted him.

We discovered he ran like an Olympic sprinter when he flew past us in a dog park. He galloped like a horse, all feet off the ground, as fast as he could, like he was in a race to win a trophy. To keep him by our side when we jogged, we fastened a red backpack on his back, weighted down with full water bottles in each side pocket. He didn't seem to mind it at all; people thought he was a therapy dog. Dante is a born runner, every night racing around the front, side and back yard of our property many times, checking on everything before coming upstairs to sleep beside us.

Dante running in the field.

Unlike many dogs, Dante is not food driven. He would rather have love and attention. He's developed this gentlemanly habit of waiting to eat his dog food until I sit down and put a fork in my mouth pretending to eat. If I don't sit down, he will stand in front of his bowl for up to a half-hour, and then lie down without eating.

He loves performing tricks and quickly mastered the one called "Flip it" that his neighbor companion Emma taught him, when she was a little girl. First, she'd say, "Sit." Next she placed a treat on the middle of his nose while holding his head straight with her hand under his chin. She gently removed her hand and said, "Flip it!" At first, Dante didn't know what to do and would jerk his head to the side; the treat invariably fell to the floor. After a few days of repetitive practice, he learned to push his head in a way that made the treat fly high, and he'd retrieve it while in the air. Now, when he wants to do this trick, he stands silently pointing to the kitchen drawer where his treats are kept.

I learned his subtle ways of communicating. Whenever he wants something to eat, he nudges me softly, looks straight at me with his alert brown eyes, walks right to his dog dish, and points at it until I put food in the bowl. Sometimes he fixates for hours on a bird that gets caught in one of our front or back porch skylights. In a nanosecond after he spots a gecko or baby rabbit, he finds it, picks it up, brings it to me, and lays it down at my feet. I praise him with a thank-you and/or pat on the head, whether the creature is dead or alive, to let him know I understand his way of showing his love.

Enjoying each other's company

In the past eight years, Dante has grown to a powerful, lean 65 pounds from the emaciated 45-pound dog we first fostered. He is not an alpha dog, but gentle, kind, and laid back. When he hears a knock at the door, he retrieves one of his favorite soft stuffed animals from his toy basket, takes it to the person, wags his docked tail, and waits to be petted. He never growls at anyone; only a couple times have I heard him bark at overly aggressive dogs. He is loving, and when he snuggles next to me, he purrs and purrs like a cat.

My neighbors acknowledge him first when I take him for a walk. Conversations usually go like this.

"Hi Dante! How are you today Dante? You know you are very handsome and love attention, don't you?"

My grown kids comment, "Mom, you have a village of people helping with Dante: a dog runner, pet nanny, vet, groomer, and friends who come over to play with him. You didn't have that many people helping raise us."

Dante with pals at exercise class

I say, "Yes. He's our family now and I like having a member, who doesn't want money or talk back. I really love 'The Dante' and emphasize 'The' to make it clear he's extraordinary." That is why I engraved on his dog tag, 'I am loved.' We are connected at the heart and we are interconnected with nature. He's helped me to be more patient, understanding, spiritual, and compassionate.

We couldn't be happier than we are that we rescued him. I often say to the Dante, "Thanks for rescuing me, too." ❀

The Red Carpet

I walk the long red carpet that extends from the curb up the steps into a grand living space filled with happy, vital women, and scrumptious food and wine. Everyone is dressed in intriguing costumes that reflect one of the year's Oscar-nominated films.

This is no Halloween Party. It's Oscar Night in Austin, Texas in 2014.

More than twenty-five women have attended these incredible annual parties for over a decade. Each year, I look forward to creating a fun, striking costume. I love envisioning, designing, and making it. I savor figuring out what materials to use, finding those that will work best, and putting on the final touches. The entire process can take weeks. Lots of pictures are taken. We eat, drink, and watch the Oscars on a huge flat screen and hope our Oscar ballot nominating the actual Oscar winners will have the most correct answers in the twenty-four categories.

This year, the Oscar costume winner was a woman who came as Olaf the Snowman from Disney's animated fairy tale musical *Frozen*. The runner-up was the *Lone Ranger* from the action western movie of the same name. Three times since I've attended, I've won for Best Costume: in 2007 for *Milk*; in 2010, for *Black Swan*; and in 2012, for Richard Parker the tamed tiger in *Life of Pi*. All three of the winning costumes I created without having seen the movies prior to Oscar night.

Milk - 2007

119

Though only two prizes are awarded each year—one for Best Costume and one for most correct answers on the ballot—we all feel that we are winners at our Oscar extravaganza. ✿

Black Swan - 2010

I love creating my
Oscar Party costumes.

Life of Pi - 2012

The IV League

*M*y fingers tremble and my heart pounds fast as I open the envelope containing my quarterly pathology reports. I hope they are short, a good indicator the results will be good. I quickly skim the findings and look for what has become my favorite word—"unremarkable"—meaning no progression since the last scan. When the report is about my brain, that word hardly captures my exhilaration.

I live from scan to scan, in three-month gulps, hoping my current treatment regimen will keep my cancer at bay until the FDA approves the next breakthrough drug. So far I've been lucky because I've been on the cusp of the newest drug being released for my type of cancer. When there is a new drug available, I can take a deep breath, knowing I have a chance to stay alive longer.

In 2006, when my diagnosis changed from Stage III to Stage IV, I realized I needed to talk to others who were in my situation. I joined an advanced cancer support group sponsored by the Breast Cancer Resource Centers of Texas (BCRC). Called the IV League, which unlike that other Ivy League, is a league no one aspires to be in. I envisioned a group of women with sunken, gaunt faces looking sick and sad. I thought, *If I qualify for an end-stage cancer group, that means I could actually die.*

Entering the meeting room for the first time, I hear the women laughing and talking about what they did over the weekend, their kids, new shoes, normal stuff, like any group of women. Sue, who had called me earlier to explain what the group is all about, greeted me warmly and said, "Welcome Deena."

The other ladies motioned for me to sit on one of the chairs in the circle with them, making me feel welcome right away. One commented, "We know this is the group no one wants to join, but we are here for each other."

After the informal introduction, the check-in started. One by one, we took a ten-minute sand hourglass, tipped it up, then gave an update on what's happening with our cancer, including the treatments, the drugs, our doctors, how we're feeling, and whether we need any kind of help. When the sand has moved to the bottom, we pass the hourglass on to the next person. Each listens intently to what the other says. No one interrupts. After check in, we open the floor to any questions or comments.

One of our former guiding lights, Jeanne, a brilliant professor, did not like to use the timer. She would simply lay it horizontally on her lap and talk until she stopped, which usually was about ten minutes. She knew so much about cancer, none of us minded because we learned so much from her. Jeanne also had the rare distinction of not only having breast cancer, but ovarian as well, which she got after she'd lost her ovaries. We couldn't believe this could happen. But it did to Jeanne.

During the first couple of meetings, I didn't understand the breast cancer lingo—ascites, paracentesis, necrosis, neuropathy, chemoflage—terms unfamiliar to me. The advanced cancer drugs sounded foreboding and it seemed ironic that many—Xgeva, Xeloda, Zometa, Zofran—started with the last letters of the alphabet. An alien in the cancer world, I felt like I was on another planet. I had resigned my job in the corporate world and was out of my element. I felt I didn't fit anywhere.

A few days later, Sue called me again and said in her soft-spoken way, "I understand what you are going through." She said, "Know I care. If you need me, I'm here." I kept on going to group and sooner than I could ever have predicted, I learned the cancer-speak terminology and about more cancer drugs for Stage IV than I ever knew existed.

We meet weekly and are connected at the heart, serving as lifelines for each other when we need support or a shoulder to lean on. Whether or not we have friends and family, we find it comforting to have each other. There's nothing like having others understand my situation, ladies who are on the same road. We are not alone. In-group, we feel safe and normal, though our "normal" is about dealing with our changing diagnoses, treatments, anxieties, fears and death. We've learned to accept the reality that we'll always be in treatment until the end.

We all agree that a vital part of managing our cancer is to have oncologists with whom we feel a mutual respect and a high level of trust. I've been lucky to have two incredible oncologists. After my first doctor moved to a clinic in Washington State, I did a lot of research and discovered my recent one, Dr. Beth Hellerstedt. Like Dr. Tucker, she too is brilliant, forward-thinking and comes up with personalized treatment solutions. I feel her genuine commitment to my wellbeing, and I love her fashion sense. She cheers me up right when I see her coming into my examining room wearing one of her stunning pairs of five-inch stiletto heels.

We often joke about cancer in our group. A member, Sandy, who has passed, came up with an idea for a Stage IV Cancer Academy Awards Show. Her wit made all of us laugh time and again with her sense of humor. Some of the imaginative awards she came up with included:

- Lowest tumor-marker number when cancer is raging throughout the body (a phenomenon that seldom happens)
- Surviving the worst allergic reaction to a drug
- Having the highest level of denial and still leading a reasonably functional life
- Living the longest while eating a crappy diet because that's all that stays down

I love making the ladies laugh too. To new people in the group, I like to say, "I may forget my American Express Card, but I never leave home without my Cancer Card. It works in places where they don't take American Express, like waiting in lines at the post office, in stores, almost anywhere." Then I share with them that I turn my wig half way around when I'm in a long line and people in front motion for me to go before them.

Another time, when driving out of the airport parking lot, the attendant requested my husband's license, which of course I didn't have. I thought fast, flipped my wig and said, "I'm Brent." The guy was so startled he motioned me to move on through the exit. Since Brent had registered the rental car in his name and his flight got delayed, I looked at the directory, saw the car stall number listed next to his name, found the car, got in and drove it."

The ladies are candid and make interesting comments. Some I remember:

"Did you notice that the first question usually asked when you check into chemo or radiation is, 'Has your insurance changed,' rather than 'how are you doing today?' That makes me want to go postal."

"My hair is gone again with my newest chemo drugs. Guess I'll dress like a monk. Go incognito. Why not? It's Austin."

The IV League

"I wish living in cancer land was like being in Disneyland where everything is magical, not so unpredictable."

Other comments are hard to digest:

"I called in hospice. I've picked out my final resting place. I will miss you all."

"My oncologist said I've exhausted all possible drugs. This is it for me. I hate wondering which day I'm going to die."

"I find myself including a disclaimer when I try to discuss my impending death with my family. Because I don't want to upset them, I say that when my time comes, 'years from now of course,' I want to be cremated."

One of our members, Val, died before I finished this story. Her death hit me really hard, not only because she was a good friend, but also because she had the same breast cancer type as I have. She had been on morphine for a month before she died. The tumors on her spinal cord sheath couldn't be radiated anymore and were pressing on her nerves. Her pain became unbearable. She only had the use of one hand as her legs and other hand became immobile. Her cancer drugs stopped working. Together with her partner, John, and her doctor, they decided to call in hospice, which is when we knew this could be the end of the road for her.

Of the seven women who came to group the first day I attended, all have died except two of us. In the years since then, more than 50 who've joined have passed. This is a reality of the IV League. The statistics in early 2014 stated, "Only one out of five who have Stage IV live beyond five years after diagnosis." I am lucky to be one of them.

Every time a cancer friend dies, it gets harder, not easier. The reality of death smacks me in the face once again; I realize I could be the next one. I go through a range of emotions: loss, sadness, joy that I was lucky to know the person, and anxiety that the next funeral could be mine. I promise myself, *Each day I will make a point to spread kindness and love. Each day I will do what I can to make someone's life easier. I will not take the simplest thing for granted; every moment is a blessing.*

I wouldn't be honest if I didn't admit there have been times when the never-ending chemo, the effects of the drugs, and seeing my friends die wear me down. I know that death is inevitable, but living with advanced cancer isn't at all like the commercialized pink ribbon life. With this cloud looming over me, there's seldom a day that I don't wake up thinking, *Whew, I made it through another night. I'm not dead yet. I'm going to squeeze in as much living today as I can.*

I'm blessed for the bonds I've developed with the IV League women. I'm blessed I've lived for eleven years since my first diagnosis, nine of the years with Stage IV. I will never give up, because if I do, I would die. Then it would be hard to live with myself. ❧

On the Run

$\mathcal{T}$he rhythmic thud of my running sneakers on the sidewalk is a familiar sound—Thump Thump Thump Thump—one I've enjoyed for decades. It's like African drums beating. I'm in my tempo. A light drizzle is falling, a breeze is blowing, and houses on each side of the street are lit up inside. No one is out this evening. It's just Dante, my loyal dog, and me. I feel his steadfast presence next to me as he runs to the pace I've set.

Thirty-six years earlier, I had the idea to run while walking around the path on the Lake of the Isles in Minneapolis with my three-year-old daughter, Jessica. An inquisitive little girl, she loved to pick colorful flowers, sit on rocks, and inspect any moving creature that caught her eye, like a lizard or a caterpillar. I loved being outside in nature and taking walks with her, but I was constantly worried, anxious and stressed about my life.

The runners on the path looked carefree, dynamic and strong. I thought running might give me a way to cope more easily with what at the time seemed insurmountable pressures: a new job at Honeywell, the death of a close friend, and my impending divorce. Jogging might be a way to run out of my skin, away from my problems, if just for a while, and maybe someday I'd look back and realize my life worked out the way it should have. I thought, *This could be the outlet to hold everything together.*

At first, I could hardly run around half a block. I ran out of breath so fast. But each day, I noticed I made it a little further when I started out slow, not fast. Eventually, I could run around an entire block, then two, then several, and finally, I plowed through that elusive first mile. I jumped up and down with joy. While running, I paid attention to my gait, my breathing, my shoes, the uneven sidewalks, and street names, things other than my issues. I pushed myself beyond where I thought I could go.

My daily runs gave me a sense of freedom, exhilaration and calm, the time to come up with creative marketing ideas for my job, the ability to go wherever I wanted, to explore new trails and neighborhoods. I could think what I wanted or not think at all. With no one telling me what to do, I could be alone in the moment and notice nature and life happening around me. I ran in every kind of weather, even pounding rain and heavy snow. I ran so fast sometimes I felt like I was flying freely, conjuring those happy memories I had years ago flying on the painted horses of the carousel.

After I'd been running for four years or so, I began to compete in 10K races. Once, I even ran Grandma's Marathon in Duluth, Minnesota, a scenic 26.2-mile course along the North Shore of Lake Superior. The night before I ate gobs of pasta to store an ample supply of carbs. The next morning I was standing in a pack of thousands of runners when the starting gun went off. It took me a while to get to the start line as I was far in the back. It was like being in rush-hour traffic, except there were no lanes.

I welcomed the exhilaration of running with a sea of humanity, listening to the cheering of the onlookers and reading the words on the backs of the T-shirts people wore. I wound up behind an eighty-year-old woman. Her T-shirt said, "I may be old but I'm ahead of you." I laughed, but it sure motivated me to step up my pace and run beside her for a while. I was blown away that she could run so fast and talk without breathing hard.

Speaking of age, in one of my races—the Bonnie Bell 10K in Minneapolis—I signed up in the age group younger than me because I didn't want my real age published the next day in the race results section of *The Minneapolis Tribune.* I was surprised when I came in third. I realized I might have come in higher in my own age group, maybe have taken first place. I hated that I couldn't camouflage my age and win at the same time.

Today I'm just as dedicated to running as ever. To be honest with myself, I'm addicted, and less concerned about people knowing my age. I reflect on my youth, middle age, and now growing older. I'm much happier now than when I was younger. And pleased that my daughters are dedicated runners too.

Over a lifetime of pounding the pavement, I wore my knees out. I had a gel-like substance injected in them to replace the loss of cartilage. Because it's synthetic cartilage from a rooster's comb, it backs up my droll comment, "I've got something to crow about."

My gait is much slower than when I was in my thirties, but nothing can stop me from running. I keep on going. I have so much living yet to do. ✤

Running into the future

"My mission in life is not merely to survive, but to thrive; and to do so with some passion, some compassion, some humor, and some style."
–Maya Angelou

Acknowledgements

*T*his book would not have been possible without the consistent support of my incredible husband. At times when I was too sick to write—due to my never-ending cancer treatments—Brent would take diligent care of me and calmly say, "Just rest now. And don't worry." His nurturing words kept me going. I love and appreciate him so much!

What a lucky day when a mutual friend introduced me to a talented storyteller, Annie LaGanga, known for her outrageous and funny true stories with The Grown Up Lady Story Company. Annie, also an author and writing coach, helped me forge a path to retrieve parts of my life I had either forgotten or blocked out, so I could re-experience those times again, and write a memoir. Her sage advice made this happen, "Take me there. Let me feel and see your experiences. If you aren't exactly sure of something, it's okay to say that. Just keep writing. Keep writing."

Those who helped in the writing of this book, deserve special recognition, including: Nancy Gore, Rose Potter, Mary Butters, Chuck Flammang, and Jack Tucker. I value their contributions and wisdom.

A big thanks to my brilliant editors, Katherine Catmull and Danielle Hartman Acee, for copy editing and proofing this book. Their keen eye for grammar accuracy, sentence structure, stylistic consistency, and everything in between, polished this memoir into tip-top shape. Thanks to Rebecca Byrd Arthur for her artful, whimsical book cover design and execution, as well as her expert design and layout of the inside of book.

I am most grateful to my family for confirming my memories of our childhood, especially Gerry Compton and Janie Montgomery. They were there for me and still are. And to my daughter, Jessica Flammang, and stepdaughter, Katie Flammang, thank you so much for your constant support. I love you more than you can imagine.

Deep appreciation and thanks to photographers, Bill Bastas and Philip Rodgers, for the professional photos they took. Thanks also to those who sent me photos including: Julie Smith, Janice Parrish, Paul Pashiban, and Nancy Hoover.

To my friends, colleagues, and cancer sisters, who have all in some way made a difference in my life, I thank you from the bottom of my heart.

Last, but certainly not least, thanks to my knowledgeable oncologists— Dr. Tom Tucker and Dr. Beth Hellerstedt—whose spot-on, proactive treatment plans, have kept me alive with Stage IV cancer. I am blessed beyond words for them, for my life, and the chance to finish this memoir.

Finally, to anyone whose name I've unintentionally left off, thank you.

CPSIA information can be obtained
at www.ICGtesting.com
Printed in the USA
FSOW03n0515150116
15560FS